The Guinness Guide to
FORMULA ONE

Ian Morrison

The Guinness Guide to

FORMULA ONE

Ian Morrison

GUINNESS BOOKS

Editor: Honor Head
Design and Layout: Eric Drewery
Picture Editor: Alex Goldberg

Published in Great Britain by Guinness Publishing Ltd,
33 London Road, Enfield, Middlesex

Typeset in 10½/12 Linotron 202 Palatino
by Fakenham Photosetting Ltd, Fakenham, Norfolk
Printed and bound in Italy by
New Interlitho SpA, Milan

'Guinness' is a registered trade mark of Guinness Superlatives Ltd

British Library Cataloguing in Publication Data
Morrison, Ian, *1947–*
    The Guinness guide to Formula One.
    1. Formula 1 racing cars.   Racing, to 1988
    I. Title
    796.7'2

ISBN 0–85112–348–1

Half title page: Alessandro Nannini's Benetton captures the thrill and colour of Formula One.

Title page: One of the success stories of the 1980s, the Benetton team.

Contents

Picture Credits

Alfa Romeo (Great Britain) Ltd; 66/67, 68. All Sport/ Vandystadt; 26, 27 (top), 28 (top), 30/31 (top), 32 (bottom), 34/35, 36 (bottom right), 39 (top), 42, 43 (top), 47 (top), 51, 53, 54 (top), 55, 59, 63, 72, 74/75, 80 (bottom), 83, 85, 94/95, 99, 102, 103 (bottom), 111, 114/115, 118/119, 120, 123, 126, 130, 131, 133, 134, 136, 137, 138/139, 142 (top), 144, 146/147, 148 (bottom), 149, 152, 154/155, 163, 167, 168, 170 (bottom), 174/175, 178, 179 (top), 180, 182/183, 186/187, 191 (top), 193 (top), 198/199, 209 (bottom), 210, 211, 214/ 215, 218, 219. Archiv Fur Kunst Und Geschichte; 9, 13, 16 (bottom), 76, 92, 156/157, 160, 176. Ferrari (Italy); 10, 11, 22/23 (top), 203. Graham Gauld Public Relations Ltd; 43, 129 (top right), 191 (bottom). Images Colour Library; 73. Keystone Collection; 17 (top), 21, 24, 36 (bottom left), 40, 42 (top), 44, 45, 54 (bottom), 88, 89, 92 (top left), 93, 96, 97, 98, 100, 101, 103 (top), 104, 105, 106, 109, 112, 169, 189, 193 (bottom), 194, 195 (top), 196, 201, 209 (top). Mercedes GmbH; 12, 14, 15, 64, 65. C.S.S. Promotions Ltd, 135, 140. National Motor Museum; 16 (top), 17 (bottom), 22, 23 (bottom), 47 (bottom), 57, 69, 70/71, 78 (top), 82, 86/87, 93 (top right), 107, 108 (bottom), 142 (bottom), 143, 148 (top), 195 (bottom), 197. Popperfoto; 204, 205, 206, 207, 212, 213, 216, 217, 221. Sporting Pictures; Half title page, Title page, 27 (bottom), 28 (bottom), 29, 31 (bottom), 38/39 (bottom), 46, 50, 58, 77, 78 (bottom), 80 (top), 84, 108 (top), 117, 158/159, 166, 170 (top), 171, 172. John Townsend; 62, 79 (top), 110, 113, 116, 121, 125, 127, 128 (top left), 128 (bottom right), 132, 141, 150/151, 153, 179 (bottom). Vintage Magazine Company; 6/7, 33, 90/91, 184/185.

1. The History of Formula One

What is Formula One? Quite simply, it is the first division of the motor racing world. Saloon car racing, Formula Three, Formula 3000, sports cars, stock cars and hill climbers are all a very integral part of motor racing, but for sheer excitement and spectacle, there is very little to compare with the roar of the high-powered Formula One cars.

Strictly speaking Formula One has only existed since the creation of Formula Two just after the last World War, but its origins lie in the very first motor races of the last century. From the moment man built his first car he has had an insatiable desire to go faster, break records, and race competitively. From the moment the first motor vehicle was produced it was inevitable that racing would soon evolve. Little, of course, did our Victorian counterparts realize that the likes of Nelson Piquet, Alain Prost and Nigel Mansell would be hurtling around some pre-built circuit at speeds approaching 200mph (321kph). But nevertheless speed is, after all, relative and the speeds reached in those early days were just as spectacular as those reached by the Ferraris and McLarens of today.

The first motor car with an internal combustion engine appeared in Paris in May 1862 and was built by Etienne Lenoir. M. Lenoir could never have foreseen how he was going to change the way of the world when he put together his first vehicle at his factory on the Rue de la Roquette. His 'car' was powered by a 1½ litre engine which ran on liquid hydrocarbon fuel. It was nearly eighteen months before

Lenoir plucked up the courage to take his first vehicle out on to the public highway, and public curiosity was soon followed by an order from no less a person than Czar Alexander II of Russia.

The motor car had arrived, and technical advances worldwide were rapid. Petrol driven engines soon followed and by 1888 Karl Benz was one of the biggest manufacturers of motor cars with his German factory, while by the turn of the century France was the leading car producer, followed by the United States, Great Britain and Germany.

Each nation took great pride in its product, and racing against rival manufacturers was a way of proving the car's worth as well as gaining national pride. The first race, as such, was over the 201 miles (323km) from Green Bay to Madison, Wisconsin, USA in 1878 and was won by an Oshkosh steamer. Whether that can be classed as the first 'motor car race' is open to argument. Another dubious claim belongs to Count Jules Félix Phillippe Albert de Dion de Malfiance who won a 19.3 mile (31.1km) race in Paris in 1887. His winning speed, believed to be around 37mph (59kph), was attained in a De Dion steam quadricycle.

However, there can be no disputing the triumph of Emile Levassor who won the Paris–Bordeaux–Paris race in June 1895. His win was in a 'real' motor car: a Panhard-Levassor two-seater with a 1.2 litre Daimler engine developing 3½hp, and this must surely be acknowledged as the first 'motor' race.

Paris was the centre for many road races, with

Previous Page: A print capturing the action from the second Indianapolis 500 in 1912.

Left: The first great series of motor races started in 1900 with the introduction of the Gordon Bennett races with this handsome trophy as the prize.

Right: A programme from one of the early city-to-city races that were popular at the turn of the century, before the start of Grand Prix racing.

cars either racing around the city or using it as a base, for example, the Paris–Bordeaux race. With the number of races increasing, more manufacturers were born, all of whom wanted to show the world that their cars were better than their rivals. With so many races being organized it was necessary to draw up a set of racing rules. This was put together in time for the 1898 Paris–Amsterdam–Paris race and, whilst crude, were necessary in order to classify the large number of different makes of car. The first motor racing rules simply divided cars into two categories, lightweight and heavyweight. Those weighing more than 882lb (400kg) were classed as heavyweight.

Car manufacture was a matter of national pride and each country wanted to produce the best car in the world. The famous Gordon Bennett series of races, which started in 1900, were designed to find out which was the best car-producing nation. The rules of the races stipulated that all parts of each competing car had to be made in the country of origin, and each country was allowed one three-car team.

The idea for such a series of races came from American newspaper magnate Gordon Bennett, the owner of the *New York Herald*. Whilst on a business trip to Paris he was fascinated by the growing interest in motor racing, and he put up the magnificent trophy to promote the motor car industry.

The first race was from Paris to Lyons in 1900

Left: Christian Lautenschlager driving the massive Mercedes to victory in the 1908 French Grand Prix at Dieppe.

Right: Alessandro Cagno of Italy on his way to victory in the inaugural Targa Florio in 1906.

1906 Iᵃ TARGA FLORIO

Alessandro Cagno su Itala

and the first three places were occupied by the French-made Panhard.

Winning suddenly became so important that it over-rode the safety element. Cars became bigger, as did engines, with the inevitable consequence that there were a lot of accidents. After the abandonment of the 1903 Gordon Bennett race from Paris to Madrid because of so many accidents, racing was taken off the open roads and put on to enclosed circuits like the one at Athy in Northern Ireland.

Gordon Bennett eventually became disillusioned with the politics of car racing and after the 1905 race at Auvergne in France he withdrew his trophy and turned his attentions to sponsoring a flying race instead.

Even without the series motor racing continued to thrive and at Le Mans in 1906 the first Grand Prix was staged. Organized by the Automobile Club de France, the drivers set off at 90 second intervals and had to cover 12 laps of the 64.12 mile (103.18km) circuit over a two day period. Also the organizers imposed a weight limit of 2204lb (1000kg). The eventual winner after more than 750 miles (1206.97km) of racing was the Hungarian Ferenc Szisz in his red Renault.

Perhaps appropriately, the first Grand Prix was held in France and won by a French car, because the French regarded their country as the home of motor racing. Consequently Szisz and his Renault had confirmed the nation's standing

in the car industry. However, a glance at the list of entrants made a French win a good bet: ten French manufacturers entered 25 cars, three Italian and German manufacturers each entered three cars. There was not a single entry from Britain or the United States.

Grand Prix racing had arrived which, unlike the Gordon Bennett races, were for individual cars, not teams of cars representing countries. However, there was still no such thing as Formula One.

When the French Grand Prix was held again in 1907 a fuel formula was introduced and cars were restricted to 50.8 gallons (231 litres) which was equivalent to 9.4 miles per gallon. The following year further restrictions were imposed; this time engines were required to have a piston area not exceeding 117sq.in ($755cm^2$) and the minimum weight of the car had to be 2534lb (1150kg). So, after two years of Grand Prix racing, formulae were laid down for the control of the sport.

In 1908 Christian Lautenschlager won the race in a Mercedes. This happened to be the last French Grand Prix for three years. The fact that the Germans had beaten the French in their 'own back yard' had little to do with the decision to discontinue the race ... well, it might have had some bearing! However interest in racing as a whole started to decline and as the ever increasing cost of producing racing vehicles spiralled many manufacturers were forced to pull out of the sport.

There was little Grand Prix racing in Europe between 1909–11 but the great road race, the Targa Florio (established 1906) continued during this period of decline.

Grand Prix racing came back to life in 1912, the year after the Americans launched their Indianapolis 500 race at the Indianapolis raceway. The Europeans had paved the way for Grand Prix racing and they weren't going to let the Americans steal all the glory. So, in 1912, the French Grand Prix was revived, and France had the pleasure of seeing one of their cars, a Peugeot, winning the race at Dieppe.

More restrictions had been placed on the Grand Prix car. This time the maximum width of the chassis or bodywork was restricted to 69in (175cm) and for the 1913 season the fuel supply was limited to 14.12mpg; streamlined tails behind the petrol tank were not permitted; and the minimum weight was reduced to 1760lb (800kg).

Early Grand Prix cars were not very different from the city-to-city cars as used in the Gordon Bennett races. But with a new style of racing there was a need to advance technically and the whole sport owes a great debt to Swiss engineer Ernest Henri, who designed the cylinder head layout for the 1912 Peugeot which became the basis for all high performance engines.

It was in the years before the First World War that manufacturers used Grand Prix racing as a form of advertising. The Sunbeam company, for example, increased its profits five times during its four year involvement with Grand Prix racing, from 1910 to 1913.

The Spanish Grand Prix was inaugurated in 1913 and in 1914, with motor racing's ever growing popularity, there was the need to standardize the sport with simpler rules than those previously introduced. The one main rule that has affected the sport ever since was the fixing of the cylinder capacity.

Top left: Christian Lautenschlager in one of the 4½ litre Mercedes that dominated the 1914 French Grand Prix, the first race under the 'new' formula.

Top right: Ready for the off at Avus in 1922 . . .

Right: A Mercedes driven by Werner at the Nurburgring in the 1920s.

Right: Just one of the many Bugattis that appeared in Grand Prix racing in the 1920s. This is the type 37 that was regularly seen in 1925.

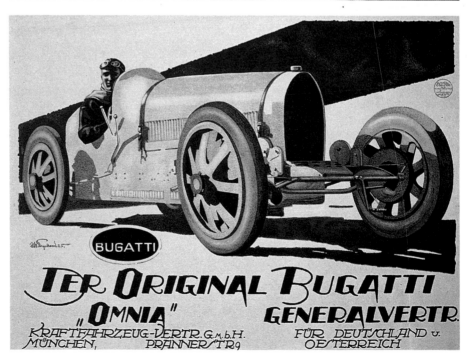

Some of the superbly built Mercedes and Benz cars that were so dominant in motor sport between 1906–39.

Left: 1906 Mercedes (11,084cc).

Left: 1909 Benz 200PS (21,504cc).

Below left: 1914 Mercedes (4483cc).

Below right: 1924 Mercedes (1986cc).

Left: 1934 Mercedes
Type W25 (3364cc).

Left: 1937 Mercedes-
Benz Type W125
(5663cc).

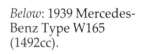

Below: 1939 Mercedes-
Benz Type W165
(1492cc).

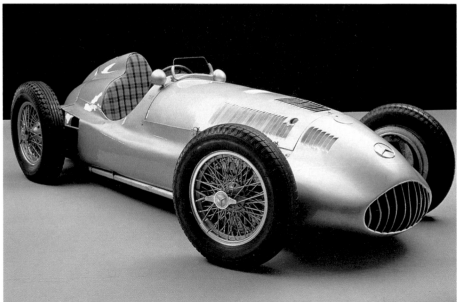

The first fixing of engine size restricted the swept volume to 4½ litres and this new 'formula' was seen for the first time in the French Grand Prix at Lyons in 1914. It turned out to be the last major race until after the war, but the French provided a spectacle for the rest of Europe to revel in. France spent a fortune on promoting and staging the race only to see Christian Lautenschlager, Louis Wagner and Otto Salzer fill the first three places in the German built Mercedes. This had a special significance, as the Mercedes engine was technically superior to its French counterpart and a few months later these same powerful engines were to be seen and heard in the German fighter planes.

After the hostilities motor racing picked up where it had left off and manufacturers continued to use the sport as a means of promoting their product and increasing profits.

In 1921 there was another change to the Grand Prix 'formula'. Engine size was limited to 3 litres and the weight limit was dropped back to 1760lb (800kg) – it had been increased to 2425lb (1100kg) for the 1914 French Grand Prix.

The international committee for motor clubs formed a sub-committee in 1922. Their sole purpose was to supervise Grand Prix racing and make sure it was run to a standard set of rules. They were known as the Commission Sportive International (CSI).

Popularity in motor racing grew as other countries followed France and Spain in staging Grands Prix. Belgium staged their first race in 1925 when Alberto Ascari senior won at Spa in an Alfa Romeo, averaging 74.56mph (119.98kph). The following year saw the birth of the German and British Grands Prix. These major races became known as *grandes épreuves* – the Formula One races of their day.

Above: Tazio Nuvolari in an Alfa Romeo at Monaco in 1932. In the period leading up to the war both driver and car were invincible.

Left: Mercedes dominated the front row of the grid before the start of the 1935 Spanish Grand Prix at Lasarte. They dominated the race as well, occupying the first three places.

In 1926 Rudolf Caracciola won the German race at Avus in a Mercedes while the inaugural British Grand Prix (known as the RAC Grand Prix) was won by Robert Senechal and Louis Wagner in a Delage at an average of 71.61mph (115.24kph).

That first British Grand Prix was raced over one of the truly great racing circuits, Brooklands. One of the first purpose-built enclosed circuits, it was situated near Weybridge in Surrey, and was regarded as the 'home' of British motor racing up to the outbreak of the Second World War.

Technical advances had seen the introduction of the supercharger by Fiat in 1923 when they built the Fiat 805, an 8 cylinder model. Like the turbocharger more than 50 years later, teething problems were encountered, but once they were ironed out, the supercharger soon became very much part of motor racing.

The post-war years saw a tremendous boom in the motor car industry and racing was, once more, seen as a way of promoting the industry after its decline during the war years. Grand Prix racing was not the only form of racing to attract a lot of attention. The Le Mans 24 hour race for sports cars was inaugurated in 1923 and four years later one of the sport's classic races, the Mille Miglia, was born. All forms of motor sport were used by manufacturers as a promotional drive for their products.

During the 1920s there were many changes to the Grand Prix formula which would enable sports cars to compete alongside their Grand Prix counterparts in the early years after the war. Between 1922–24 engine capacity was reduced to 2 litres and the minimum car weight was down to 1433lb (650kg). The rules also stipulated that each car should carry two occupants, one being a travelling mechanic, but their

Left: Two of the greats of the 1930s, Rudolph Caracciola (leading) being pursued by Tazio Nuvolari, the eventual winner, during the 1936 Hungarian Grand Prix at Budapest.

Below: The Type 51 Bugatti which won the 1931 French Grand Prix at Montlhery.

combined weight was not to be less than 264lb (120kg). Otherwise they had to carry ballast! In 1925 the riding mechanic was dispensed with as cars became more mechanically sound, but his seat remained.

For the 1926 season engine capacity was down to 1½ litres and minimum weight was reduced even further to 1322lb (600kg); this weight limit was increased to 1543lb (700kg) the following year and cars could either be one- or two-seaters.

There were major and significant changes in 1928. All restrictions on engine size were removed but cars had to be between 1212–1653lb (550–750kg). Race distances were also fixed for the first time, and had to be at least 373 miles (600km) in length. Further 'tinkering' with the formula in 1929 saw car weight altered once more. This time it was to a minimum of 1980lb (900kg), and fuel restrictions limited the supply to 14.5mpg.

From the years just before the start of the First World War to the latter part of the 1920s the number of major races had increased but by 1928 interest in the sport by individual manufacturers had dwindled. Like all forms of 'advertising', Grand Prix racing had served its purpose, and the need to use the sport as a means of increasing profits was no longer viable.

From 1928 to 1931 the sport picked up momentum again, largely due to the smaller cars being eligible for Grand Prix racing. This time the interest came from the private enthusiast, and not the manufacturers. It became largely an amateur sport with wealthy enthusiasts funding their racing operations out of their own pockets. One such enthusiast was Ettore Bugatti. His cars, with the familiar horseshoe-shaped radiator became legendary in the 1920s and 1930s. His Bugatti type 35 was a classic and is credited with more than 2,000 wins. Bugatti, and the 1½ litre Delage, were the last of the truly great two-seater racing cars.

In the years leading up to the Second World War the big manufacturers returned as motor racing was used as a propaganda platform. Fascist support led to State encouragement for the Italian Alfa Romeo team who were developing new cars, particularly after the lifting of all formula restrictions in 1931 to an open 'Formula Libre'. Bodyweight limits were re-introduced in 1934 (max. 1653lb/750kg) and, not wishing to be outdone by Mussolini, Hitler offered public funds to the Mercedes and Auto Union teams.

The 1934–37 weight limit meant that every conceivable part of a car had to be lightened. Thus, cars like the C Type Auto Union were capable of developing in the region of 600bhp.

Both Italy and Germany sought to gain superiority on, and off the race track and in the years between 1934–39 the two countries dominated the sport. The Italian Alfa team initially had the upper hand and proved their superiority at Montlhery in 1934, filling the first three places in the French Grand Prix with Louis Chiron taking the chequered flag. But the Germans then took control and the Mercedes and Auto Unions were first over the finishing line in most Grands Prix. Even after the formula changed to a maximum engine capacity of 4½ litres unsupercharged and 3 litres supercharged in 1938 the Germans remained invincible.

Just before the war Enzo Ferrari, the man behind the Alfa Romeo team, turned his attentions away from the grandes épreuves to voiturette racing, Grand Prix racing's second stream.

Voiturettes had been in existence since before the First World War, initially with a 3 litre engine capacity. But in the inter-war years a 1½ litre limit was imposed. Voiturettes were raced largely by amateurs and races were generally shorter and less demanding than the grandes épreuves. By the mid-thirties voiturettes had a racing calendar of their own. Ferrari had foreseen that in the immediate post-war years, with finances being tight, the 4½ litre Grand Prix car would be too costly to run, and voiturettes would therefore capture the imagination.

Ferrari started producing his own special voiturette just before the war and at Leghorn in 1938 he showed off his masterpiece to the racing world – the Alfa Romeo Type 158. With its 8-cylinder 1½ litre supercharged engine, pointed tail and tubular frame, the Alfetta (as it was known) was to become a classic.

In its first race Alfettas occupied the first two places at Leghorn. At last, Italy had dethroned the Germans. The Italians liked winning again and to make sure it stayed that way they changed the rules. Quite simply, they said that any race in Italy must be for voiturettes only!

By the time the 1939 Tripoli Grand Prix came around, the Alfa team was confident of a victory. The Germans were represented by Mercedes who, little known to the Italians, had quickly developed a voiturette that was better than the 158. To everyone's surprise, the superior engineering of the Germans dominated and Mercedes finished 1st and 2nd with one of the Alfas a long way back in 3rd place.

Right: The 1939 Tripoli Grand Prix which the Germans dominated thus gaining a psychological advantage over the Italian Alfas before the outbreak of the war.

The deadliest of rivals on the racing track, France and Germany were soon to be rivals again, but of a different and bloodier kind. The race at Tripoli was the Italians' last chance before the war to get the better of their German rivals.

After the Second World War the Italians regained their domination of the track. The Germans, however, were not allowed to take part (anyway, the Auto Union factory was behind the Iron Curtain in the Eastern Zone, and Mercedes' Stuttgart factory lay in ruins after enemy bombing). They were to rise again, but initially their priority was to build vehicles for use in the construction industry as Germany was rebuilt.

Before the war was over, the Fédération Internationale de l'Automobile (FIA) was formed out of the old Alliance Internationale des Automobile Clubs Reconnus (AIACR), but they left control of the sporting side to the CSI.

As anticipated, with the shortage of money and fuel, it was a couple of years before Grand Prix racing returned to its peak of the pre-war years, but on 9 September 1945 the roar of the engines was heard once again in a one-off race at Bois de Boulogne when Jean-Pierre Wimille won the Grand Prix de la Liberation in his Bugatti.

Racing returned to Nice, Marseilles, Albi and Geneva, with the Maseratis showing an early dominance. Early post-war races were run under Formula Libre rules with sports cars racing alongside the Grand Prix cars.

In 1946 a new formula was fixed for Grand Prix cars. Supercharged cars would have a swept limit of 1½ litres while unsupercharged engines could be up to 4½ litres. The FIA ruled that this formula should exist until the end of 1952 when it would be reviewed, so manufacturers of the day had plenty of time to develop their new cars. The new rules suited British manufacturers who had been specializing in voiturettes since the 1930s, and the likes of Raymond Mays' supercharged ERA (English Racing Automobiles) in particular would become more competitive.

If 1946 was a significant year in the re-birth of Grand Prix racing after the war it was an equally sad one because it saw the passing of the great Brooklands circuit. No more would the great Bugattis be seen speeding around the famous track. Brooklands was requisitioned by the Vickers aircraft company during the war, and was then sold to them in 1946 for £300,000, which resulted in the closure of one of the sport's most famous venues. But with Brooklands dead, there was still plenty of life left in Grand Prix racing and the sport underwent its greatest period of change.

International Grand Prix racing returned in 1947 with races at Pau, Spa, Milan and Bremgarten (Switzerland). The Italians took advantage of the lack of German opposition – this time Alfa was challenged by the rival Maserati team.

On 2 October 1947 the FIA held their annual meeting and announced that from 1948 there would be two Grand Prix formulae. The existing grandes épreuves would be called F.I.1 and a new formula, for cars of 500cc supercharged or 2 litres unsupercharged, would be called F.I.2. Thus Formula One was born.

Despite the FIA's names for the two formulae, the main formula continued to be called The Grand Prix Formula, while the new formula was known as Formula Two. Many sources referred to the two as Formula A and B.

Changes were certainly blowing through the motor racing world and in Britain in particular there was a new breed of car racer, the club enthusiast. At the end of 1949 a new 500cc class of car was given international status. This was to be known as Formula Three. The first international race for this new formula was the Paris Grand Prix at Montlhery in 1950, won by Carter in a Cooper.

The first race under the title of International Formula One race was also in 1950. It was the Pau Grand Prix on 10 April won by Juan Manuel Fangio in a Maserati. Two months earlier the FIA decided that it would run a world championship for drivers based on results in the leading Grands Prix, starting with the British Grand Prix at Silverstone on 13 May.

So, after nearly 50 years of Grand Prix racing, we can at last answer the question: 'What is Formula One?' It is, as you will have seen, the premier form of Grand Prix racing. It always has been, even though it was never previously known by that name. It may well not have been born until the late 1940s but it would be impossible and unfair to have used that as our starting point. Formula One started the moment the Gordon Bennett races commenced at the turn of the century, albeit under a different guise. But once Formula One arrived it was to herald the start of the golden days of Grand Prix racing.

In the latter years before the war technical advances, such as the new non-leaf suspension, helped make cars faster. Consequently they demanded the best drivers. The new world championship era was to bear that out more than ever.

Sadly the likes of Jean-Pierre Wimille, killed in a voiturette race in 1949, were no longer with us. The great Nuvolari was reaching the end of an illustrious career. But there were new men like Fangio, Ascari and Farina ready to take over from their famous predecessors.

In brilliant sunshine at Silverstone on 13 May 1950, 21 drivers lined up for the start of the first world championship race, the British Grand Prix. It was a carnival atmosphere, and a day of great national pride. The King and Queen, and Princess Margaret, attended the meeting and chatted to drivers in the pits before the race. Organized to perfection by the Royal Auto-

Left: The 'Tank-type' Bugatti 57. Seen here during the 1936 French Grand Prix at Montlhery with Jean-Pierre Wimille behind the wheel. He went on to win the race.

Right: Jean-Pierre Wimille in his Alfa Romeo during a wet Italian Grand Prix at Turin in 1948. Wimille won the race; sadly the great Frenchman was killed at Buenos Aires the following year.

mobile Club, the large crowd eagerly awaited the race.

Alfas were back to the fore after taking a year off from racing in 1949 to concentrate on building road cars. They occupied the front row of the starting grid, and that was where three of them stayed as they filled 1st, 2nd and 3rd places thanks to Farina, Fagioli and Parnell.

The first world championship season was dominated by Alfa drivers who won six of the seven championship races. The only one they didn't win was the Indianapolis 500, which formed part of the championship until 1960, but which remained an American domain; very few European drivers made the trip to Indianapolis each May. Italian Giuseppe Farina was crowned the first world champion after winning the final race of the season, the Italian Grand Prix at Monza.

Meanwhile Enzo Ferrari had left Alfa to set up his own Ferrari racing team, and in 1951 it was his team that took the spotlight away from the long-standing supremacy of the Alfas. Ferrari had developed a full 4½ litre unsupercharged car the previous season. The Alfas dominated the early part of the season, but in the British Grand Prix at Silverstone, Froilan Gonzalez steered one of the big Ferraris to victory. That was the start of a winning career for the now famous Italian manufacturer which has continued for more than 37 years.

Ferrari completely dominated the championship in 1952 and occupied the first four places. But the season saw dramatic changes to Formula One. Sadly, gone were Alfa Romeo who, realizing they were no longer a match for the new supremos of Italian car manufacture, pulled out of the sport after failing to acquire

Above: Maurice Trintignant in the Ferrari 625 which occupied 2nd and 3rd places in the 1955 Argentine Grand Prix.

Right: Jim Clark in the Coventry Climax V8 powered Lotus 33.

Left: Two of the greatest names in motor racing Jim Clark (enclosed in the flower decoration!) and Colin Chapman (right). Sadly both men are no longer with us but their memory will last forever.

much needed capital from the Government for the development of a new car.

But the big change in world championship racing was the switch from Formula One to Formula Two for the 1952 and 1953 seasons. This meant all cars were racing to the 500cc supercharged/2000cc unsupercharged limits. This two-season formula gave manufacturers time to prepare for the 1954 season when a new 2½ litre/750cc formula was coming into force.

Ferrari had developed a 4-cylinder 1980cc unsupercharged version of his early sports cars. The Tipo 500 was to dominate world championship racing in the years of Formula Two. In 1952 they won every round of the world championship (except the Indianapolis 500) and in 1953 it was virtually the same story with the exception of the Italian Grand Prix won by Juan Manuel Fangio in a Maserati.

The Italian domination of the world championship was threatened by the return to Grand Prix racing of Mercedes Benz in 1954. Their fuel injected straight-eight 2496cc engine was to power the W196 to victory in the French Grand Prix with Fangio, the man who was to dominate world championship racing for the next five years, behind the wheel. Fangio was that season's champion as Ferrari and fellow Italian Maserati had to go back to the drawing-board.

Mercedes still dominated as Enzo Ferrari sought a way of counteracting their charge. He developed a shorter chassis car – the Tipo 553, a lead which was soon followed by other manufacturers. Gone were the days of the great rambling machines. Racing cars were now starting to take the look of the sleek slimline machines we know today.

Mercedes withdrew from Grand Prix racing at the end of the 1955 season in the wake of the Le Mans disaster when one of their cars flew into the crowd killing more than 80 people. Their exit paved the way for the Italians to re-take control, which they did via Maserati and the new Lancia-Ferrari team which came about when Enzo Ferrari put in a successful bid for the financially struggling Lancia company.

In 1957, for the first time in more than thirty years, British teams gained Grand Prix recognition through the Vanwall team of Tony Vandervell by scoring two Grand Prix wins, at Pescara and Monza, with Stirling Moss in control. But

Britain's ultimate moment of glory was still to come.

Oil companies put pressure on the CSI in 1958 to introduce compulsory use of 100–130 octane commercial aviation fuel as opposed to ordinary pump fuel which they wanted the use of to help boost their own industry. The CSI gave way to their request but it posed problems for some manufacturers who had to modify their engines. One such manufacturer was Vanwall, but Vandervell carried out successful modifications on his engines and his cars swept to the newly instituted Constructors' Championship after winning six championship races.

Rear-engined cars made an impact in 1959 with Jack Brabham winning the world title in a Cooper-Climax. Enzo Ferrari was soon to latch on to this simple development and modified his Dino 246, but it was the Cooper-Climax which remained the outstanding rear-engined car of the day. However Enzo Ferrari was no fool and he had spent time preparing a car ready for the new 1½ litre formula that was being introduced on 1 January 1961.

The new formula, which imposed greater restrictions than ever before on the Grand Prix car, limited unsupercharged engines to 1500cc, stipulated a minimum weight of 992lb (450kg), insisted on all fuel being pump fuel and made roll-over bars, self-starters and double braking systems compulsory. Not happy with that, it was further ruled that no oil could be taken on during a race, and that no wheels could be enclosed by bodywork. With that lot to contend with, it was perhaps inevitable that a man of Ferrari's talent would be the first to dominate when the new formula was introduced. And that is just what he did.

His Tipo 156 won five championship races and clinched the manufacturers' crown for the Italian manufacturer. The British constructors were left behind as Ferrari got on with the job of producing a car to fit the new formula. BRM had lodged an appeal with CSI against the new formula and, so confident were they of winning, they did nothing about developing a new car. When they lost the appeal they realized that they should have had the same insight as Ferrari. However, Ferrari's success was shortlived. After a disagreement many top men, including manager Romolo Tavoni, walked out on the Italian magnate, creating an unforeseen opportunity for British cars to capitalize upon Ferrari's demise, which they did.

BRM, who had been threatening since 1949 to take Grand Prix racing by storm, won the Constructors' Championship with the type P57, and provided the world champion, Graham Hill.

The much improved lighter chassis carried a V8 engine capable of producing 190bhp, and it was to prove too good for the rival Coventry-Climax powered Lotus developed by the late and great Colin Chapman.

The CSI announced that it was extending its 1½ litre formula beyond its initial three years (1961–63) by another two years. This was encouraging news for the British manufacturers who were beginning to show the world they were supreme at building these smaller cars. It was particularly good news for Lotus.

Chapman started a revolution the rest of the motor racing world would soon follow when he hit upon the idea to build his Lotus 25 with a monocoque frame. His simple idea, which surprisingly nobody had thought of before, was, in effect, to sit the driver in between two frames. Gone was the multi-tubular frame chassis, and in its place were two long aluminium sheets formed into boxes joined together with transverse steel bulkheads and cross members. As a result the driver was set lower in the car and the chassis became lighter.

Ferrari returned to the fore with their semi-monocoque Tipo 158 in 1964, and put an end to the British charge. It also thwarted the challenge of a new manufacturer, Honda, with its transversely mounted 12-cylinder engine.

The 1965 season saw the end of the 1½ litre formula, as Lotus, Colin Chapman, and Jim Clark went out in a blaze of glory winning the drivers' and constructors' titles. The honour of winning the last 1½ litre world championship race, however, went to Honda with their RA272

at Mexico City. In the forty-seven Grands Prix under the 1½ litre formula, Jim Clark won nineteen races, and the Coventry-Climax-powered Lotus a staggering twenty-two.

Two years earlier the CSI had announced that from 1966 the next limits would be 3 litres unsupercharged and 1½ litres supercharged. Would the British challenge be as strong or would Ferrari come back? The answer was simple . . . neither would!

The British manufacturers were hit by the shock announcement in 1965 that Coventry-Climax would no longer be producing their engines, and consequently they were totally unprepared for the new 3 litre formula. Ferrari were certainly well equipped with their V12 engine, for so long used in their sports cars, but it was the Brabham team who showed the others the way.

After an unsuccessful start to the new season with an old Coventry-Climax engine they teamed up with Australian company Repco who produced a 3-litre V8 engine. The engine, while not as powerful as some of its rivals, was simple and reliable. The chassis designed by Ron Tauranac was also one of simplicity. That was to be the key to Brabham's success. The new formula also increased the original weight limit of cars to 1102lb (500kg), and all race distances were restricted to 186–248 miles (300–400km).

Weight limits were increased to 1168lb (530kg) in 1969 to accommodate fire extinguishers, defined roll-over bars and safety fuel tanks. The increased use of aerodynamic aids came under close scrutiny and restrictions were placed on

Left: Cars like the Ferrari Tipo took the sleek-looking racing car into the 1970s.

Right: The 1973 world champion Jackie Stewart in his Cosworth-powered Elf-Tyrrell.

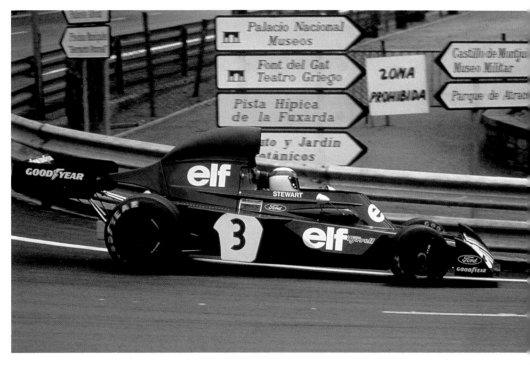

Below: Ken Tyrrell has certainly been an innovator and his six-wheel Project 34 in 1976 was far from a gimmick.

their use. A limit of 12 cylinders was imposed. So, while the engine capacity remained unaltered, several new changes affected the sport.

Brabham-Repco had continued their success story in 1967 but 1968 belonged to Team Lotus who, despite losing Jim Clark in a Formula Two race at Hockenheim, won the Constructors' Championship and Graham Hill won the drivers' title. The Lotus success was centred around Ford-Cosworth who supplied engines not only to Lotus but to the McLaren team and Ken Tyrrell's new Matra outfit.

Cosworth won all Grands Prix in 1969 but in 1970 Ferrari returned to the winner's podium with the sleek and magnificent looking 312B with its 12-cylinder flat engine and improved semi-monocoque chassis made of small-bore tubing.

As the formula remained unaltered into the 1970s it saw the great Jackie Stewart become the new hero of the sport behind the wheel of Ken Tyrrell's first Formula One car to bear his own name. The early seventies also saw a heavy involvement of sponsors as never seen before.

Large public companies used motor racing as an advertising platform. And it was not just motor industry allied companies, but non-associated companies like cigarette and cosmetic manufacturers who saw motor racing as a powerful form of advertising. The sport had always been a popular spectator sport but now it was becoming a popular television sport and this appealed to potential sponsors.

This boom started in 1968 when Lotus had their cars painted in the colours of John Player's *Gold Leaf* brand of cigarettes. The days of the traditional national colours, green of Britain, silver of Germany and red of Italy, were long gone. Now, it was a question of sponsorship being needed in the sport, and in return, sponsors should get their money's worth. Advertising on cars was the best way to repay them.

Many despaired at Lotus's action, but it was a harsh reality that commercialism and sponsorship was creeping into sport, and was a much needed tool. *Autosport* asked in 1968: 'Should interested firms wish to advertise their products in this way the benefits to motor racing generally outweigh all other objections.' That was the start of the commercial boom.

Lotus were 'market leaders' once more in 1971 when they introduced their 56B gas turbine car, the sport's first turbine powered engine.

The 1973 season saw one of the many rows

Above: In the shortened Spanish Grand Prix at Montjuich Park on 27 April 1975 Lella Lombardi of Italy made Formula One history when she became the first woman to pick up points in a world championship race. She finished 6th in her March.

Below left: The Renault turbo engine . . . the start of the great turbo revolution that hit Grand Prix racing in 1977.

Below right: The modified Renault RE20 in 1980.

that, sadly, have since hampered the sport. It was between the newly-formed Grand Prix International (formed by the circuit owners) and the Formula One Constructors Association (FOCA). Prize money was the centre of the disagreement. FOCA wanted a substantial increase in prize money; GPI only offered 12½ per cent. Agreement between the two was only partially reached, but eventually FOCA came to an agreement with each individual organizer which thwarted a possible cancellation of some or all of the calendar.

FOCA and the CSI were also at loggerheads over the possible introduction of two-heat races designed to reduce fuel loads. But agreement was reached in time for the start of the season. Further squabbles continued once the season got under way and the Grand Prix Drivers Association (GPDA) expressed displeasure at the use of Zolder for the Belgian Grand Prix. The race was threatened for a time because of the unsuitability of the track, but it did eventually take place.

By the mid-1970s cars took on a design not dissimilar to those of today. The low chassis and rear aerofoils were common to most cars and these designs were to set the pattern for all subsequent cars.

Just as 1973 was hit with problems before the start of the season, so was 1974. This time a fuel crisis nearly halted all forms of motor racing. However the programme went ahead; only the South African Grand Prix was cancelled. But once racing got under way the CSI had another problem to face ... cutting down the fields to suit each race.

Many new manufacturers had come into Formula One racing and it would have been foolish to let every entrant compete. However, the CSI and FOCA agreed that each race should be limited according to each circuit's suitability, and this figure should be arrived at by a series of qualifying practice laps.

In basic car design there was little change in 1974 and 1975: as far as winning was concerned, the triumphant years of the Ford-Cosworth were over as Ferrari returned with their 312T, complete with transverse-mounted gearbox.

The control of motor racing was gradually slipping away from the CSI as was clearly demonstrated in 1976 when FOCA persuaded the CSI to change its rules concerning the use of aerofoils and restrictions of wheel-rim and tyre widths, thus showing how powerful the Formula One Drivers Association had become.

One of the most interesting developments of the 1976 season was the launch of the Tyrrell Project 34 six-wheeled car. Initially believed to be a publicity stunt, Ken Tyrrell was deadly serious, and when Jody Scheckter steered it to

victory in the Swedish Grand Prix at Anderstorp, the racing world no longer treated it as a joke.

By 1977 most off-season activity centred around the drivers, just as it does today: 'Who will drive for whom next season?' is the most asked question, long before the final chequered flag of the season has fallen. But on a technical front there was another six-wheeler. This time it was the March but, unlike the Tyrrell of the previous year, its four wheels were at the rear.

The other major technical advance of 1977 saw the launch of the *John Player Special* Lotus 78 with its new design aimed at improving down thrust and thus preventing as much air as possible from passing under the car. It became known as the 'wing car'. The racing car was constantly being changed as manufacturers sought to improve speeds and road holding, as well as maintaining safety standards.

The 1977 British Grand Prix saw the return to Grand Prix racing of the French manufacturer Renault. But this time they brought with them the sport's first turbocharger. Like the supercharger before it, the turbo failed miserably and the doubters had cause to 'celebrate'. Within a couple of years, the 1492cc Renault engine had been modified so much its output was up from 510bhp to 1300bhp. And in 1979 the car had its first win when Jean-Pierre Jabouille steered it to victory in the French Grand Prix.

The biggest influence on the sport for the next decade had arrived. Suddenly manufacturers were converting to turbo-charged engines as it became the latest in a long line of innovations in Grand Prix racing. Turbo-charged cars have, of course, since dominated the Formula One scene and men like Nelson Piquet, Alain Prost and Niki Lauda have all won world titles in turbo powered cars.

Following the turbo invasion, the next biggest modification to the Grand Prix car was the ground effects revolution. Following the lead by the Lotus 78 in 1977, other manufacturers were redesigning their cars to reduce the drag under the car. Consequently chassis were lowered, and skirts were fitted to the sides to keep any air under the chassis without escaping through the sides. By 1980 most teams were racing ground-effect cars. The effect meant that, amongst other benefits, cars could take corners and bends at greater speeds.

Further squabbles between FOCA and the Fédération Internationale du Sport Automobile (FISA) (the successor to CSI in 1979) in the early 1980s nearly split Grand Prix racing and, indeed, the public arguments between Bernie Ecclestone (FOCA) and Jean-Marie Balestre (FISA) were well documented at the time. FISA wanted to

ban ground-effect cars; FOCA were totally against such a move. Because of the fall-out between the two bodies the 1980 Spanish Grand Prix did not eventually count towards the championship although it was run and won by Australian Alan Jones.

The arguments raged on into 1981 and when the first race of the season got under way at Long Beach, cars were adhering to a new 2¼in (6cm) static ground clearance rule. Modified suspension systems, however, rendered the cars less safe than when they had full skirts. FISA wanted the removal of the skirts to make the cars safer! In 1982 skirts and systems used to fill the gap between the bodywork and the ground were banned completely.

With the banning of skirts manufacturers had to have a rethink on suspension systems and 1987 saw the birth of 'active' suspension – a sophisticated computer system of regulating the

Above: Gone were the skirts but the Grand Prix cars of 1982 still retained their 'ground effect' as this Ferrari shows.

Right: The ATS of Hans Stuck and the McLaren of John Watson clearly show the use of skirts in 1979.

height of the car's ride under all conditions of braking, cornering and acceleration. It is one of the biggest advances in Formula One racing since Colin Chapman's ground-effects car ten years earlier.

Fuel capacity restrictions were re-introduced in 1984 with a limit of 48 gallons (220 litres). With the average turbo getting around 4mpg, it was plain to see that careful use of the accelerator was needed. Victory was not assured to the fastest car or driver, but to the most frugal. In the opening race of the season Patrick Tambay was coasting to a guaranteed 3rd place at Rio when suddenly his car ground to a halt on the last lap. It is embarrassing enough running out of petrol on a motorway, but to do it on the last

lap of a Grand Prix in front of millions of watching eyes . . .

With no change to engine size limits since 1966 the sport's governing body announced plans in 1986 for the phasing out of turbos to be completed by the start of 1989 with a return to a 3½ litre limit for which all cars must have normally aspirated engines. To try and give the non-turbo cars an equal chance, it was announced that in 1988 turbo cars had to have approximately 300bhp clipped off their race tuned engines and their fuel tank capacities reduced to 33 gallons (150 litres). The non-turbo cars had no fuel restrictions and their minimum weight limit was 88lb (40kg) less than the turbos. However, this did no good as Marlboro-

McLaren, with their Honda V6 turbo, dominated the season winning the Constructors' Championship with a record number of points.

We have seen over the years that changes in formulae have often brought changes in teams' fortunes. The McLarens of Prost and Ayrton Senna completely dominated the last 'turbo' world championships. But how will they fare in 1989? Will Ken Tyrrell enjoy glory days again like those of the late 1960s and early 1970s? These questions will soon be answered.

But one question we have already answered as we have sped through more than eighty years of Grand Prix racing is: 'What is Formula One?'

Formula One is the premier category of motor racing. It will always maintain that status. But what changes the future holds there is no knowing. Driver and manufacturer will constantly have a desire to go faster. Consequently designs will change in the future. But happily, the organizers, drivers, and manufacturers of the most exciting sport in the world are fully aware of the need to be safety conscious. Because of that, Formula One motor racing will continue to draw its vast army of followers.

The racing car of today looks very different from the giant Alfas, Mercedes, Ferraris and Auto Unions of the pre-war days. But the cars and drivers of today have the same appeal as they did fifty years ago. The goal is still the same: to be faster than the next man; to be faster than the next car.

Right: The driver's view . . . 1920s style.

Next page: Grand Prix racing 1988-style . . . Ivan Capelli in his familiar blue Leyton House March.

Left: There is no finer sight than Grand Prix cars racing away from the starting line, as they are here at the beginning of the 1988 Portuguese GP.

Below: The Benetton team is a recent but much applauded addition to the Formula One circuits.

2. Manufacturers and Their Cars

The manufacture of a racing car has been described as 'model-making on a grand scale': the Grand Prix car is nurtured and looked after by men in the same way boys look after their toy cars.

Since the early days of motor racing, the sport has been used as a platform. Initially it was to promote the motor car industry, then taken over by wealthy and enthusiastic amateurs, and before the last war it was used as an arena of propaganda as the German manufacturers, along with funding from the Third Reich used the sport to gain a psychological advantage over their fellow protagonists, Italy.

After the war, and once the world championship was inaugurated, it became more competitive and, like many sports, the Baron de Coubertin belief of 'Taking part is the most important' had long gone. Winning is the name of the game and never more so than in motor racing. Grand Prix racing is a kind of warfare as one team strives to produce a car faster than any of its rivals. And in a technological world often measured by the thickness of a tissue paper the success of these expensive toys breeds not only success but money.

Sponsorship is the backbone of the motor racing business and success guarantees renewed sponsorship which means continued cash in the bank, an essential commodity when one needs a £20 million budget to run a two-car Formula One team. Engines alone cost in the region of £40,000, and top drivers don't come cheaply these days.

Left: The McLaren M14A at the 1970 Race of Champions, driven here by Peter Gethin.

Below left: The man who started one of the most successful Formula One teams, Bruce McLaren.

Below right: Twentieth century technology is very much part of the McLaren operation, and computers are used for most aspects of the business including timekeeping.

Above: Grand Prix racing is not all glamour . . . somebody has to clean the tyres!

In an era of multi-million pound salaries it is not only the team owners and drivers who reap the rewards, the top designers and engineers also receive large sums commensurate with their skills as they help to produce a car capable of outpacing and outlasting the opposition. Because of the need for constant change and improvement, a top engineer's salary has risen from approximately £20,000 ten years ago to the six figure mark today. Most of the leading engineers are British.

Drivers are only as good as the cars they are given, but a good car driven by a bad driver will never win races; it is therefore a package of the two. However, the real 'race' takes place before the starter's flag falls; it is the race to beat the next team with a new technological advance.

On-board computers are commonplace in modern-day racing cars as the driver has to stay in constant touch with his mechanics in the pits. The computerized technology sends back details of the car's performance to the pit men who are constantly making decisions which they relay to the driver over the two-way communication system.

Computers also play their part in car design to ensure a driver's safety and comfort. Cars are built around the driver these days but care is taken to ensure that he can eject from his cockpit in under five seconds in a case of emergency. One feature of the modern-day car is the removable steering wheel for making access from the vehicle a lot easier. The sight of a driver making his way back to the pits with his steering wheel in hand is not an uncommon sight on the Grand Prix circuit these days.

The design of the racing car is in the hands of skilled engineers and designers who have the added help of computer technology. Cars are undoubtedly much safer today, as indeed are race tracks, and safety must always remain motor racing's first priority.

Over the next few pages we shall look at all the 1988 Grand Prix teams; how long they have been in the sport, what success they have had and so on. We will also take a nostalgic look back to the early days of the world championship when the all-time greats such as Alfa Romeo and Mercedes Benz dominated proceedings. In addition, the teams in the interim period who have made an impact, like Honda, Surtees and of course Renault with their turbocharger, will not be forgotten.

First let us start with the current teams.

Above: Emerson Fittipaldi was McLaren's first world champion in 1974.

Right: Stefan Johansson of Sweden had a season at McLaren in 1987. He is seen here driving the TAG-powered MP4/3.

Grand Prix Racing Teams 1988

The 1988 season was the last season for the turbo-powered engines. It had been eleven years since Renault launched their RS01 amidst a host of doubters. Within a few years many manufacturers were running turbo-charged cars, and eventually, all turned to the new power units. But now the turbo revolution has ended as normally aspirated cars become the norm again in 1989.

Eighteen teams took part in the 1988 world championship and we will use them as the starting point as we look back on the many manufacturers who have participated in this great sport over the last 80–90 years.

Undoubtedly the most outstanding team in 1988 was **Marlboro-McLaren**. Now stalwarts of more than 80 Grands Prix, the team was founded in 1966 by Bruce McLaren who followed in the footsteps of fellow Australasian, Jack Brabham, by forming his own team.

The genius of McLaren as a constructor started in 1963 when he formed Bruce McLaren Racing Ltd. The company produced highly successful Can-Am and Tasman Cup cars and the first McLaren, a modified 2½ litre Cooper, made its debut in the 1964 Tasman Cup. However, with financial support from BP and Firestone he ventured into Formula One in 1966 with the Robin Herd designed McLaren M2. It made its debut in the opening race of the season at Monaco and McLaren himself put the car on the fifth row of the grid. Sadly, the race ended after ten laps due to oil problems.

The car picked up its first points in the British Grand Prix at Brands Hatch a couple of months later, but their first win did not come until the 1968 Belgian Grand Prix when McLaren was behind the wheel of his M7A complete with the successful Ford-Cosworth engine. By now the McLaren car also had a great reputation in North America after winning on its Can-Am debut at Elkhart Lake in 1967. In total, McLarens won a

record 48 Can-Am races, including a staggering 23 in succession between 1968–70. The team suffered a tremendous setback in 1970 when boss McLaren was killed while testing a Can-Am car at Goodwood; however the team kept going and the following season they introduced the Ralph Bellamy designed M19A.

Having established themselves as one of the leading teams in 1973 with the Gordon Coppuck designed M23s they were to enjoy their best season a year later. Emerson Fittipaldi joined the team from Lotus and McLaren attracted lucrative sponsorship deals from Texaco and Marlboro. The team still enjoys that relationship with the cigarette manufacturer today. Fittipaldi clinched the world title and McLaren took the Constructors' Cup in 1974. James Hunt, in the M23 Cosworth, provided the team with its second world champion in 1976 when he had a narrow win over Niki Lauda. However, Ferrari pipped McLaren for the Constructors' title that year.

It was eight years before the team added another championship. But in 1984, after switching to the Porsche engine, they swept to the Constructors' title by a massive 86 points. The team's two drivers, Niki Lauda and Alain Prost dominated the world title and only half a point separated the two men at the end of the season with the title going to the Austrian. Since then McLaren have been outstanding, with the exception of an intrusion from Williams in 1986 and 1987. Prost won the world title in 1985 and the Constructors' Cup was back in the team's trophy room thanks to the TAG-Porsche V6 turbo engine.

Team boss Ron Dennis commissioned John Barnard to create the carbon fibre MP4/2 which carried Alain Prost to four wins and a second world title in 1986. Barnard moved to Ferrari that year and his replacement at the Woking factory was Gordon Murray from Brabham. The 1987 season belonged to Williams but the following year it was McLaren's turn to dominate Formula One racing.

As teams were preparing for the normally aspirated return in 1989, McLaren continued with turbo power, this time with the Honda engine, which had carried the Williams to such prominence a year earlier. The McLaren-Honda combination was invincible as drivers Prost and Ayrton Senna completely dominated the season. They won the first eleven races of the

championship as they took the team's all-time total beyond the 65 mark, a figure bettered only by Ferrari and Lotus.

Ferrari is the longest established of all current Formula One teams, and is unquestionably the biggest name in motor racing.

Enzo Ferrari, the man whose name is synonymous with motor racing, died in 1988 at the age of 90. Although his health had been failing in later life, he still played a crucial role in the running of the company. And one of 'Il Commendatore's' last tasks was to persuade Britain's Nigel Mansell to join the giant Italian team. Ferrari had tried to get another great British driver, Stirling Moss, in the 1950s, but had failed. That was one of the biggest disappointments of Ferrari's life. Perhaps Mansell will bring back the glory days to the Ferrari team, and so write a belated epitaph for the great man.

Enzo Ferrari was himself a racing driver, after failed careers in sports journalism and opera singing. He joined the Alfa Romeo team in 1920 and finished second in the Targa Florio. But his skills were soon diverted away from the track on to the drawing board. His organizing skills helped turn Alfa into the top team of the era but when they pulled out of racing in 1929 he took over their factory producing cars under the Scuderia Ferrari banner although these were basically Alfa-designed cars. The first true Ferrari was introduced in 1947 and by the time the world championship was launched in 1950 the Ferrari had gained a reputation for being a reliable single-seater.

Soon the Ferrari was the 'star' attraction whenever it started a race and the black prancing horse motif, taken from the emblem of First World War fighter ace Francesco Paracca, became the best known trademark in motor racing.

Alfa Romeo were back on the scene by 1950 and dominated the inaugural world championship but at the British Grand Prix a year later the giant Ferrari of Froilan Gonzalez saw the chequered flag to give the car the first of its record 94 Grand Prix wins. Because of the company's reputation they have been able to recruit top drivers and Alberto Ascari (1952–53), Juan Manuel Fangio (1956), Mike Hawthorn (1958), Phil Hill (1961), John Surtees (1964), Niki Lauda (1975 and 1977) and Jody Scheckter (1979) have all been Ferrari world champion. The company's top designers have helped the team to a record eight Constructors' Championships between 1961–83.

Ferrari has been the biggest name in motor racing since the last war and not only in Formula One. They have also produced some classic sports cars and, of course, their road cars are

---

Left: The greatest name in motor racing, Enzo Ferrari (right) seen here with Prince Bernhard of the Netherlands in 1961.

Right: John Surtees behind the wheel of the Ferrari Tipo 312 at Silverstone in 1966.

Below: Gilles Villeneuve, one of the finest drivers of the 1970s, driving the Ferrari 312T in 1979. Sadly, he lost his life at Zolder in 1982.

much sought after as the ultimate status symbol for the rich and famous. The Dino 166, named after Enzo Ferrari's late son, was one of the great sports cars of all time.

One of the company's great racing cars was the 4-cylinder 2 litre Ferrari 500 which monopolized the Grand Prix scene during the days of Formula Two competition in 1952 and 1953.

The key to Ferrari's Grand Prix success over the years has been the reliability of its engines. In recent years, however, it has been left trailing in the wake of the TAG, Honda and Renault turbos. But with turbo now gone, Ferrari could well return to the top of the sport. In the past they have taken a start on their rivals when new regulations have been introduced. With their skill and experience, they could do the same again when the new formula is introduced in 1989.

The greatest motor racing dynasty is now run by the management of the Fiat company who became involved with Ferrari in the 1960s, but the name of Ferrari will live on for ever.

Between them Ferrari and McLaren have won more than 150 Grands Prix, but if you add to them the total wins by **Lotus** then you have a combined total equal to more than half of all world championship victories since 1950.

Lotus was the brainchild of the late Colin Chapman, one of the greatest innovators the sport has seen. Chapman gave the sport ground-effect cars, gas turbine engines, big money sponsorship, and Jim Clark. The motor racing world owes a great debt to Colin Chapman. Like Enzo Ferrari, Chapman has left a legacy not only of racing cars, but of classic road cars which are collector's items.

Colin Chapman studied engineering at London University and his first involvement with racing was to modify Austin Sevens. In 1952 he formed the famous Lotus Company with £25 borrowed from his girlfriend (who later became his wife). The first Lotus car was based on the Austin chassis with a plywood body and 750cc engine which became very popular among club enthusiasts. The genius had completed his first masterpiece.

His heart had been set on Formula One from an early age and in 1958 the first Lotus Grand Prix car appeared when the Frank Costin designed Lotus 12 made its debut at Monaco with Cliff Allison and Graham Hill behind the wheels of the two entries. Allison finished sixth.

The first time a Lotus took the chequered flag in a Grand Prix was at Monaco in 1960 when Stirling Moss crossed the line in a privately entered rear-engined Lotus 18. The birth of Lotus as an outstanding Formula One team was in 1960 when Chapman and Jim Clark teamed up to form one of the sport's greatest partnerships.

Right: Innes Ireland, the top Lotus driver before the arrival of Jim Clark.

Above: Colin Chapman (left) the man who made the Lotus marque, and Jim Clark (right) the man who helped make it one of the best-known names in Grand Prix racing.

Right: The Lotus 33 which made its debut in 1964. It was basically a modified Lotus 25.

Clark went on to win a then-record 25 Grands Prix, all in a Lotus, and was twice world champion, in 1963 and 1965. Sadly their partnership came to an untimely end in 1968 when Clark was killed during a Formula Two race at Hockenheim. Shaken, Chapman realized he still had a task to perform – to produce world beating racing cars, and he carried on, even though he had lost the world's best driver and a friend.

Graham Hill lifted the gloom by winning the world title that year. Then tragedy struck the team yet again when, two years later, number one driver Jochen Rindt was killed at Monza. His lead in the world championship was so great at the time that he won the world title posthumously.

Emerson Fittipaldi in 1972 and Mario Andretti in 1978 both won the title for Chapman but the team has not had a champion since. The brilliant Brazilian Ayrton Senna looked capable of bringing the world crown back to the team after finishing third in 1987, but his move to the more competitive Marlboro-McLaren team ended such ambitions. Lotus won the Constructors' Cup five times between 1968–78, a figure bettered only by Ferrari.

Over the years Chapman was responsible for new ideas which other teams soon followed. His Lotus 25, which became a world beater, had a Coventry-Climax V8 engine. But its greatest asset was its simple monocoque construction instead of the multi-tubular space frame. Within a season most manufacturers were looking at such designs for their cars. In an eighteen month period the Lotus 25 won 18 Formula One races, all with Clark at the controls. The next great Lotus era was to come in the late 1960s after Chapman switched to the popular Ford-Cosworth engine in 1967. Had Jim Clark lived long enough to have tested the engine to its fullest, there is no knowing how successful Lotus, Cosworth and Clark would have been.

Chapman needed a successor to the Coventry-Climax engine and he turned to an ex-Lotus man Keith Duckworth for help. Duckworth, along with Mike Costin (brother of Frank) and Bill Brown had been running the successful Cosworth Engineering Company. Chapman asked them if they could produce a Formula One engine. And with the financial aid of the Ford Motor Company they produced their famous DFV (Double Four Valve) 3 litre V8

engine which became legendary in the annals of Formula One history. The engine achieved the first of its many victories on its debut at Zandvoort and the man behind the wheel was none other than Jim Clark.

Colin Chapman continued to set the trend when, in 1968, he had the team cars painted in the colours of cigarette manufacturer John Player & Son's *Gold Leaf* brand. The move was criticized but one has only to look at the money in motor racing these days to pinpoint Chapman's move twenty years ago as a day when the sport started another period of growth and development.

Colin Chapman had motor racing running through his veins. He wanted to see it grow, and he wanted personal success for his team. He was constantly looking for new ideas and in 1977 he developed his famous 'wing car' which was aimed at improving down thrust and keeping the car closer to the road. Once more, other manufacturers soon followed suit.

The motor racing world, and motor industry as a whole, was shocked and deeply saddened with the news in December 1982 that Chapman had collapsed and died. The sport lost a dear

friend and a great innovator. Happily his famous marque is so steeped in history that the name Lotus will never die.

The season after Chapman's death the team switched to the Renault turbo after a long and successful relationship with Cosworth. A further switch in 1987 to the Honda unit was expected to bring better results but Lotus is still waiting to get back to the top of the Formula One ladder.

Of the other current marques only Williams and Tyrrell have managed double figures in terms of Formula One Grand Prix successes. The **Williams** team, run by Frank Williams, has won 40 world championship races which puts it fourth behind the 'Big Three', and is just reward for the many years of efforts by the team boss.

A former racing driver of modest ability, Williams described himself as 'good on the straight . . .'. He entered Formula One in the late 1960s with no money but a big heart and a dream to match. That dream has now been fulfilled and in 1986 and 1987 his team dominated Grand Prix racing winning the Constructors' Cup both years as his two drivers, Nelson Piquet and Nigel Mansell won 18 races between them.

Above: The famous black and gold livery of the *John Player Special* Lotus was one of the best-known cars of the 1970s.

Left: Modern technology has helped in the advancement of the Grand Prix car. Here a Lotus engineer is keeping an eye on the active suspension system via his computerized unit.

Right: Frank Williams may be confined to a wheelchair following his accident in 1986 but his enthusiasm for the sport has not waned. He is seen here sharing a joke with Nelson Piquet, the last Williams' world champion.

Below: The Williams FW11B at the company's Didcot headquarters.

On 8 March 1986 disaster struck the team. The tragedy was not on the track but on a French road. Frank Williams was returning from Paul Ricard where he had been watching a testing session when his car left a nearby road and plunged down a ten-foot embankment. As the car overturned Williams took the impact on his head, breaking his back. Now paralysed from the shoulders down, Williams has not lost his insatiable appetite for working and for motor racing. He is still very much the 'boss' at the team's Didcot headquarters and has the same desire to win and build the best Grand Prix cars. His team certainly worked hard on his behalf in 1986 but in 1987 the Honda-powered Williams was invincible, and that year Frank Williams was personally honoured with the CBE in the New Year's Honours List.

Sadly, after a disagreement, their Japanese supplier withdrew their support for 1988 and the team used the John Judd built engine. After an unhappy start to the season, the new power-unit proved its worth in the second half as it competed with the more powerful turbo units. For 1989 they have teamed up with Renault but this posed problems for Williams because they use the French fuel manufacturer Elf; one of Williams' big sponsors was Mobil . . . but not any more!

Frank Williams eats, sleeps and breathes racing cars. But, although he is the head of the company, their success stems from the respectful relationship between Williams and chief designer Patrick Head. A technical genius, Head designs the most aerodynamically efficient cars on the circuit.

Williams first entered Formula One in 1969 when he bought a Brabham BT26A and privately entered it under the Frank Williams (Racing Cars) Limited name with his friend Piers Courage in the cockpit. They were rewarded with second placings at both Monaco and Watkins

Left: John Judd with one of his normally-aspirated engines supplied to the Williams team in 1988.

Glen. Courage was killed during the 1970 Dutch Grand Prix but Williams carried on with privately entered March cars for such drivers as Henri Pescarolo and Carlos Pace. A partnership with Canadian Walter Wolf in 1976 only lasted a season and in 1977 Frank set up a new company, Williams Grand Prix Engineering. They acquired a March 761 and Williams, who had taken some trusty mechanics with him, later recruited the services of the promising young Patrick Head. Williams picked up sponsorship money from Saudi Airlines and at last the career of Frank Williams, Formula One constructor, was showing an upward trend.

Head designed his first Grand Prix car in 1978, the neat FW06 powered by the Cosworth engine. Williams was successful in getting Australian Alan Jones to join the team. But it was Clay Regazzoni who drove the first Williams to a Grand Prix victory in the 1979 British Grand Prix. However, twelve months later Jones was the first of three Williams world champions. Since then Williams has been one of the most dominant teams of the 1980s and it was unfortunate for Williams that Nigel Mansell could not win the world title during his spell with the team.

The only other current manufacturer with anything like a pedigree is the **Tyrrell** team run by Ken Tyrrell. Like all great teams, there is a great man at the helm; the Tyrrell team is no different.

Tyrrell started his career by running an apprentice Formula Cooper team in 1960. He first ran a Formula One team in 1968 when he looked after the Anglo-French Matra outfit using a modified Formula Two car. A year later the team were constructors' champions when Jackie Stewart won six of the eleven races. That was the start of a great relationship between Tyrrell and Stewart.

Surprisingly Tyrrell and Stewart quit Matra at the end of 1969 when the French team announced it was going to abandon the Cosworth engine in favour of developing their own V12 power supply. Both Tyrrell and Stewart knew it would not be competitive enough and consequently moved to March.

Formed in 1969 by Max Mosley, Alan Rees, Graham Coaker and Robin Herd, the team name was made up from the initials of its founders. Their first Formula One car was the March 701 powered, of course, by the Cosworth.

Towards the end of the season Tyrrell brought from under the wraps one of the closest guarded secrets of 1970, his own Formula One car, the Tyrrell 001. There had been little indication he was going to manufacture his own car, but he

did and furthermore the man behind the wheel once more was Jackie Stewart. The car was designed by Derek Gardner who was recruited from Harry Ferguson Research.

In 1971, after a switch to Goodyear tyres, Tyrrell and Stewart took the world of Formula One by storm. Stewart won six championship races as he went on to win his second world title and Tyrrell took the Constructor's Cup. Another pair of titles came their way in 1973 with the modified 005 but tragedy struck when, during practice for the final race of the season, Francois Cevert was killed at Watkins Glen.

Jackie Stewart's retirement followed immediately and Tyrrell was no longer a serious title contender. They didn't become competitive again until 1976 when they launched their revolutionary six-wheeled Project 34 car. At first it was regarded as a piece of publicity for the Derek Gardner designed car, but those who knew Tyrrell and Gardner knew they were not out for publicity of this kind and their revolutionary car had to be taken seriously. At Anderstorp the car proved itself – Jody Scheckter finished first and team-mate Patrick Depailler second as they took maximum points in the Swedish Grand Prix. The Project 34 was certainly no joke.

But the car failed dismally in 1977, largely due to tyre problems, and for the first time a Tyrrell car went through a season without a Grand Prix win. Derek Gardner resigned at the end of the season and Maurice Phillippe took over as the new chief designer. He came up with a new four-wheel drive car, but the Ford-powered Tyrrell 008 was no match for its rivals.

The team was hit by cash flow problems in 1979 as they started the season without a major sponsor following the withdrawal of Elf and First National. During the season, however, Italian electrical firm Candy stepped in to help. Candy are now sponsors of Liverpool FC. Since then Tyrrell have languished amongst the 'also rans' of the Grand Prix world, largely because of Ken Tyrrell's loyalty to the Cosworth engine and his reluctance to switch to turbo power following the boom of the early 1980s.

In 1984 Tyrrell was to be involved in 'political' and legal wranglings after Martin Brundle's car was found to contain lead pellets in the fuel tank after finishing second in the Detroit Grand Prix. It was contended the lead would effectively increase the octane rating of the petrol. Brundle was disqualified and his early championship points were deducted. Furthermore, the Tyrrell team was banned from the championship. Tyrrell subsequently cleared himself through the courts and in 1985 the team was reinstated.

Above: Keke Rosberg in the Saudi-sponsored Williams, Rosberg was the 1982 world champion.

Left: The Matra MS10 which Jackie Stewart drove to victory in the 1969 South African Grand Prix at Kyalami.

Right: The Tyrrell six-wheeler (Project 34) was regarded as a joke but the pundits stopped laughing when Jody Scheckter steered it to victory in the 1976 Swedish Grand Prix.

Right: Ken Tyrrell, the man who has done so much for Grand Prix racing.

Below: Jackie Stewart in an Elf-Tyrrell. Stewart and Tyrrell were as synonymous as Clark and Chapman.

Midway through the season Tyrrell switched to turbo-powered engines for the first time when they did a deal with Renault, but sadly it was all too late. Shortly afterwards FISA announced their plans for the phasing out of turbos and it was back to the drawing board for Ken Tyrrell and his team. In 1987 they returned to the Cosworth V8 engine after finding the turbo too expensive to run.

Of the current Grand Prix teams, the five covered below can be likened to the top teams in the first division of the Football League. They have been dominant over the years, and are still going strong but, like the Football League, motor racing is not made up only of a few teams, it consists of all the teams. And just as the first division would not be the same without the likes of Wimbledon, Norwich and Southampton, so Formula One racing needs the support of its other teams.

It is easy to talk about winners like Everton, Liverpool and Arsenal, but what about the other teams? They play an important role and, let's face it, one would never have thought ten years ago that Wimbledon would have beaten Liverpool in the FA Cup Final. Therefore, there must always be hope for the likes of Colini, Rial, Minardi and so on.

A look at the other 1988 Formula One teams shows **Ligier** as having the best record from their twelve years in Grand Prix racing. From the moment they made their debut at the 1976 Brazilian Grand Prix they have been a regular starter in Formula One and have eight wins to their credit starting with the 1977 Swedish Grand Prix when Jacques Laffite had the honour of being behind the wheel.

Founded by the former Cooper and Brabham driver Guy Ligier, an ex-rugby player, his first car was the 1.6 litre Cosworth JS1 (the JS being dedicated to his close friend Jo Schlesser who was killed in the 1968 French Grand Prix). At first specializing in long distance sports cars, their first Formula One car was the very competitive JS5 designed by ex-Matra engineer Paul Carillo who, understandably, put a Matra engine in the new car. They remained loyal to the Matra engine until the French supplier pulled out of Grand Prix racing in 1978. Ligier then switched to the Cosworth DFV engine, having to rebuild their car to fit the new unit. The new 'marriage' was to see the team finish third in the Constructors' Championship and drivers Laffite and Depailler win three championship races. The JS11 won at its debut at Buenos Aires.

The following season, still with Ford, they finished runners-up to Williams and in 1981 after teaming up with Talbot they switched to the

old Matra V12 engine. But then things started to go wrong for the French team. It became disorganized and they were no longer producing a competitive car. They endured a troubled season in 1983. Talbot withdrew their support, Laffite and Cheever were replaced by Jarier and Bousel, and the plan to use the Renault turbo was dropped after they abandoned the Matra V12. Consequently they reverted to the now uncompetitive Ford-Cosworth supply.

In 1985 top Renault men joined the Vichy based team. By then Ligier had been using the Renault turbo but they never threatened the top teams as they did in the late 1970s. Their last win was in the 1981 Canadian Grand Prix.

The last few years have been troubled times for Ligier. Just before the start of the 1987 season Alfa Romeo withdrew their engine supply after Rene Arnoux made uncomplimentary remarks about their power unit. They got hold of the Megatron engine at the last minute. In 1988 they switched to the Judd V8 but the Michel Tetu designed JS31 was one of the biggest disappointments of the season. On eight occasions a Ligier car has taken the chequered flag. It is going to have to make up a lot of ground to add to that figure in 1989.

Like Ligier **March** has a Formula One pedigree, dating to the 1970s, but they have not enjoyed the same success as their French rivals.

The company was founded in 1969 by four enthusiasts, Max Mosely, Alan Rees, Graham Coaker, and Robin Herd. Their first car was the Formula Three March 693 which made its debut in September 1969. After deciding to venture into Formula One they recruited the services of Ken Tyrrell and six months after the Formula Three debut no fewer than five of the new March 701s lined up for the start of the Spanish Grand Prix. Two of them, driven by Jackie Stewart and Chris Amon, were on the front row of the grid. It was a remarkable achievement for the new team. Stewart, in third place, was the highest finisher but in the next race, in Spain, it was the Scot who led the Cosworth-powered car to its debut win.

Stewart and Tyrrell left before the season was out, but March remained a force to be reckoned with. However, it was not until the 1975 Austrian Grand Prix that Vittorio Brambilla gave the team its second win and the following year Ronnie Peterson won at Monza. Although that is it in terms of Formula One successes, it does not signify the end of the March story.

In the mid-1970s the company realized that it needed to diversify its interests and under the direction of Robin Herd, now a CBE, March Engineering started producing cars for CART

Jacques Laffite in the Renault-powered Ligier on its way to 6th place in the opening Grand Prix of 1985 at Rio de Janeiro.

racing in the United States. This decision proved to be the right one as March cars won the famous Indianapolis 500 five years in succession 1983–87. In 1976 however, Mosely and Herd sold the Formula One operation to ATS. Having enjoyed considerable success in Formula 3000 in 1986 and thanks largely to a sponsorship deal with Leyton House, a real estate subsidiary of a large Japanese conglomorate, the Leyton House March became the Formula One branch of March Engineering.

Under team manager Ian Phillips, a former motor racing journalist, they ran just one car in 1987 and got among the points for the first time in the Monaco Grand Prix with Ivan Capelli in the driver's seat. They expanded the team in 1988 when Brazilian Mauricio Gugelmin joined Capelli in the new Adrian Newey designed Judd-powered 881. So far their return to Formula One has not been as successful as their first venture in 1970, but they have the vast experience to put matters right.

Another team long associated with Formula One is that of **Lola** who first appeared as long ago as 1962 and returned in 1986 after a 'chequered' career.

Lola have been building cars since 1956 when designer Eric Broadley established the company. His first car of any note was the front-engined sports car with the 1098cc Coventry-Climax engine which made its debut in 1959. He followed this with a single seater Formula Junior car the following year which he produced from his small south London factory.

In 1962 Broadley was asked to produce a Formula One car for John Surtees who had the backing of the Bowmaker Hire Purchase company. Broadley developed a small and light-weight conventional multi-tubular spaceframe chassis fitted with the V8 Coventry-Climax engine. Two cars made their debut in the opening race of the season at Zandvoort. Roy Salvadori was way down the grid, but John Surtees grabbed pole position. Sadly, on lap 9, a suspension fault caused Surtees to slide off the track and Salvadori's car was withdrawn because of this apparent technical fault.

Surtees defected to Ferrari in 1963 and Broadley carried on with Formula One but without any success, and then quit the Grand Prix scene. He did not return until 1974. In the meantime however, he produced the well known Lola

Left: The Leyton House March team before the 1987 Australian Grand Prix. Driver Ivan Capelli is in the foreground.

Right: Eric Broadley returned to Lola in 1974 and produced the T370, seen here in the capable hands of Graham Hill.

Below: John Surtees in the Lola T100 in 1968.

Ford Mark 6 GT which excelled in sports car races and the success of the car and subsequent expansion of the company meant a move to larger premises at Slough.

The powerful 4.2 litre Ford powered cars took the north American racing scene by storm and in the inaugural Can-Am season, 1966, the Lolas of John Surtees, Mark Donohue and Dan Gurney won every round of the championship except one. That same year Graham Hill drove a Lola to victory in the Indianapolis 500, only the second British triumph in the great race after Jim Clark's win the previous year. Before the end of the decade Broadley was making cars for every branch of motor racing except Formula One.

Towards the end of 1973 Broadley was approached by Graham Hill to produce a Formula One car for him and he came up with the Lola-Cosworth T370 for Hill's new Embassy team. But the only point the combination picked up was for 6th place in the Swedish Grand Prix at Anderstorp. The following year Lola was out of Formula One yet again after Hill formed his own team using the Lola T370 chassis.

The Lola name that made its return to Formula One in 1986 was in fact an American team owned by Carl Haas who arrived with a lot of Can-Am experience and a fistful of dollars from a lucrative sponsorship deal with a large American food conglomerate, but the team was soon thrown into disarray when they lost their sponsors. They also had problems with the Hart engine whilst waiting for the new Ford-Cosworth, and so Lola's 'return' was an unspectacular one. The following year the next Lola team was a completely different one. This time they were French-based at Rouen, but used the Lola chassis made at their new Huntingdon headquarters in England.

The new team was formed by Gerard Larrousse, the former team manager at Renault and Ligier, who was joined by Didier Calmels to produce the Larrousse Calmels Lola team. They recruited the services of top designer Ralph Bellamy but he left the company midway through the 1988 season. Once more Lola's return was not without incident, but *was* without results.

Of the new teams to have emerged in the 1980s **Benetton** has been the most successful by far. And of all the non-turbo powered cars in 1988, they were the pick of the bunch.

The Italian knitwear company first came into Formula One in 1983 as the exclusive backers to the Tyrrell team which had struggled to find a major sponsor for two years. The team was renamed Benetton-Tyrrell. After a couple of traumatic seasons with Tyrrell, including the controversial 1984 season, Benetton ventured into the world of Formula One in their own right when in 1986 they bought the Toleman team.

With the enthusiasm of owner Luciano Benetton, team boss Peter Collins and one of the sport's unsung heroes, leading designer Rory Byrne, the Benetton team was soon to make its mark and the team is now a much respected one.

Based at Witney in Oxfordshire, England, the first Benetton, the B186 bore a striking resemblance to the last Toleman, the TG185, but with the powerful BMW turbo engine as opposed to the Hart used by Toleman. Gerhard Berger gave the team a great debut at Rio when he finished in 6th place. And it was Berger who had the distinction of driving the team to its first win at Mexico later in the season.

Rory Byrne's distinctive cars, in their famous green, yellow and red colours, have proved themselves very reliable. When BMW pulled out in 1986 they switched to the non-turbo Ford-Cosworth engine in 1987 in readiness for the return to normally aspirated engines in 1989. But they were still capable of giving the turbos a run for their money on occasion, particularly with the talented pair of Thierry Boutsen and Alessandro Nannini behind the wheels. They are certainly a team to look out for as Grand Prix racing goes into the 1990s.

Unlike Benetton, **Arrows** have been around for some time, but their first Grand Prix win still beckons. In fact, in the ten years since they made their debut at Rio in 1978, and more than 150 races later, their best finish has been 2nd, which they have achieved four times, the last occasion being at San Marino in 1985. Statistically, they have taken part in more world cham-

pionship races without registering a win than any other team.

The Arrows team was founded late in 1977 after being conceived by unhappy members of the Shadow team who were feeling the brunt of severe financial restraints. The new company consisted of, among others, ex-March co-founder Alan Rees, driver Jackie Oliver, engineer Dave Wass, and chief designer Tony Southgate. Like March before them, the team's name was made up of the initials of its founders.

Work on the first Formula One car, the FA1, didn't start until late November, but two months later it was on its way to Rio for its first Grand Prix. But that was to be the start of a troubled and controversial debut season.

One of the team sponsors, Franco Ambrosio, was jailed; Gunnar Nilsson who was contracted to partner Riccardo Patrese in the new team, was struck down with the cancer that eventually claimed his life and he never drove for Arrows, and Shadow took Arrows to court on the grounds that the FA1 was a copy of their 1978 DN9 Shadow. Arrows lost the case and were ordered to destroy their car. Fortunately Tony Southgate had another car, the A1, on the drawing board, and less than two months after the court case it was on the track.

Their next car, the A2, was aerodynamically an eye-catcher, and it attracted a lot of attention on its debut in 1979. With the new car and later the A3, the team enjoyed its most successful period. Since going into the 1980s, Arrows have suddenly been among the 'also rans'. The switch from the Cosworth engine to the BMW turbo in 1984 came too late to stop the slide and in 1987 the team switched to the Megatron engine after the company, a subsidiary of Arrows' new owners USF&G, bought the entire stock of the old BMW engines.

The team underwent major changes in 1987. Apart from being acquired by the American financiers USF&G they recruited designer Ross Brawn, formerly of Haas-Lola, as a replacement for Dave Wass.

Arrows drivers Eddie Cheever and Derek Warwick were both 'knocking on the door' on several occasions during the 1988 season, and came close to equalling the team's best Grand Prix finish. Despite their disastrous start in Formula One ten years ago, the Milton Keynes-based company are more determined than ever to get their first win under their belt.

Of the other current teams, the oldest is **Osella** who celebrated their ninth season in Formula One in 1988. After a successful spell in Formula Two they made their Grand Prix debut in South Africa in 1980 with American Eddie

The Grand Prix car is not what it appears when 'naked'.

Cheever behind the wheel of their 'kit car' powered by a Cosworth engine.

A small company operating on a low budget, team boss Enzo Osella has found the financial pressures a big handicap over the years and his cars have fared no better than a fourth placing in the 1982 San Marino Grand Prix. The team has not picked up any points since Jo Gartner finished fifth in the 1984 Italian Grand Prix.

A switch from Ford to the BMW turbo in 1983 made little difference to the car's performance, and the Alfa V8 turbo used since 1984 is no longer the power force it once was. Still struggling, Osella cut down from two to one car in 1988. They nearly quit a couple of years ago but the announcement that normally-aspirated engines were returning in 1989 encouraged Osella to stay in Formula One.

When the West German-sponsored **Zakspeed** team entered Formula One in 1985 they produced their own engine and chassis, a bold move at a time when the likes of McLaren, Williams and Tyrrell relied upon outside engine manufacturers. The first all-German team in Formula One for twenty years, the fact that four years later Zakspeed is still going strong is testament to their belief in their product, even if they are still anxiously awaiting their first win.

Erich Zakowski built his own V4 turbo engine, but sadly it has not proved to be as good as he hoped. Furthermore, no other teams have taken the engine. Gustav Brunner, the man who designed the 1987 Ferrari, joined Zakspeed in 1988 after a short spell at the small Rial team.

With 1989 going non-turbo Zakspeed didn't develop their own engine but brought the famous Yamaha name into Formula One. Yamaha developed a normally-aspirated unit for them which meant that Ferrari were, once more, the only Grand Prix team to manufacture a complete car on its own premises.

Another Grand Prix newcomer in 1985 was the Italian **Minardi**, who came straight from Formula Two to the 'big league' without any significant track record behind them. Their sole success in the European Formula Two championship was at Misano in 1981 when Michele Alboreto beat Geoff Lees and Mike Thackwell into 2nd and 3rd places.

Owner Giancarlo Minardi recruited the services of Pierluigi Martini in 1985 and the following year they introduced the talented newcomer Alessandro Nannini who, when paired with the Moderni turbo, proved to be a speedy acquisition. Minardi stayed with the Moderni engine in 1987 before switching to the Cosworth V8 in 1988, when the team's first driver, Martini, returned to replace the sacked Spaniard Adrian Campos in the Caliri-designed M188.

The AGS-BMW driven by Philippe Streiff won the very last European Formula Two championship race at Brands Hatch in 1984. The following year the team produced a Formula 3000 and in 1986 **AGS** made the natural progression to Formula One, making its debut at Monza. A heavy car, it was powered by the Motori Moderni V6 engine. It made one other appearance that season at Estoril with Ivan Capelli behind the controls.

Still using a bulky chassis AGS turned to the Cosworth DFZ unit in 1987 and signed Pascal Fabre as a replacement for Capelli. Fabre was replaced by Brazilian Roberto Moreno towards the end of the season and in the final race he finished sixth at Adelaide, the team's best finish. Their ex-Formula Two driver Streiff returned to the team in 1988.

One of a number of small teams in Formula One, AGS are based north of Toulon in France and run by Henri Julien. The initials AGS stand for *Automobiles Gonfaronaise Sportive*.

The remaining teams that played a part in the 1988 season all made their debut during the season. None had a particularly happy baptism, although **Rial** enjoyed slightly better fortunes than the other three, by virtue of their 4th placing in the US Grand Prix at Detroit, thanks to Andrea de Cesaris. Their neat, trim car was produced by Gustav Brunner, the ex-Ferrari man who left Rial during the 1988 season to go to Zakspeed. The head of the German team, known as Rial Racing, is Gunther Schmidt, who previously ran the ATS Formula One team which quit at the end of 1984.

The other three teams to be seen for the first time in 1988 were all Italian. The best known was probably the **Eurobrun** team owned by Walter Brun, the slot machine magnate better known for his sports car teams over the years.

Although the team is Swiss-owned, its Formula One factory is based at the old Euroracing workshops (which looked after the Alfa Romeo team in 1983) at Senago on the outskirts of Milan, while the Brun sports car team retained its base in Switzerland. Managed by Paulo Pavanello their first car, the ER188 designed by Mario Tolentino and Bruno Zava, was not competitive enough to make any impact in its first season and the team's two drivers, Argentinian Oscar Larrauri and Italian Stefano Modena, found 1988 an uphill struggle.

Shortly before the final race of the 1988 season, Walter Brun expanded his involvement in Grand Prix racing when he acquired the shares of the Brabham team.

Another car that made an unimpressive debut in 1988 was the **Coloni** owned by Enzo Coloni. The team made the jump direct from Formula Three to Formula One after a brief stop off in Formula 3000. Outstanding in Formula Three in Italy, they ran two cars in the 1986 Formula 3000 championship as part of their grooming for the top formula. However, they made little impact on the Grand Prix scene in their first year, despite recruiting three AGS designers. Coloni ran only one car in 1988, driven by Gabriele Tarquini but the Perugia-based company plans to run two cars in 1989.

Left: In their short time in Grand Prix racing, first as a sponsor and then as a manufacturer, Benetton has become a much respected name in Formula One.

Right: A dramatic action shot of Thierry Boutsen in his Arrows during the 1986 Brazilian Grand Prix.

Below: Alessandro Nannini in his Minardi during the 1986 San Marino Grand Prix. Team owner Giancarlo Minardi, however, prefers his drivers to keep their cars on the track . . .

The **BMS Dallara** team was another newcomer in 1988. Better things were expected of this team which had built up quite a reputation in Formula Three in Italy. The Cosworth powered F188 was designed by Gianpaulo Dallara who had previous experience with De Tomaso and Iso-Marlboro in the 1970s although this was the first car to bear his own name. Owned by Guiseppe Lucchini, the team styled itself *Scuderia Italia* but sadly it has not lived up to the reputation of the first Scuderia team, Ferrari.

This concludes a look at the eighteen teams which made up Formula One racing in 1988. No doubt there will be other new names over the next few years, and no doubt some of those covered on the previous pages will disappear. Sadly, some of the great names of motor racing are no longer with us, and it would be unfair to look solely at current manufacturers without recalling the role some of the great names from the past have played in the growth and development of Grand Prix racing.

Great Names From The Past

One name from the not-too-distant past is that of **Brabham**, although they did not enter a team in Formula One in the 1988 season for the first time in 27 years, after boss Bernie Ecclestone decided to pull out because of the ever crippling financial pressures.

The inaugural Brabham Grand Prix car made its debut at the Nurburgring in 1962 with founder Jack Brabham behind the wheel. The car, the BT3, was designed by fellow Australian Ron Tauranac (better known for his Ralt cars in recent years), and used the V8 Coventry-Climax engine. It had its first win at Rouen two years later when Dan Gurney drove the BT7 to victory.

When Climax pulled out of Formula One in 1965 Brabham turned to the Australian-made Repco engine which proved an instant success. Brabham drove the BT19 and 20 to four championship wins in 1966 and clinched his third world title. In 1965 the team also won the first of its two successive constructors' titles.

Tauranac was one of the last designers to turn to the fully monocoque chassis when he built the BT33 in 1970. Brabham enjoyed success in the new car but he was 44 years of age at the time and thought it time to retire, so he hung up his helmet and returned to Australia. Ron Tauranac bought Brabham's shares in MRD (Motor Racing Developments Ltd), and in 1971 Bernie Ecclestone, an ex-Formula Three driver, bought the company outright. The Ecclestone/Tauranac partnership didn't work and Tauranac left in 1972.

Ecclestone closed down the production side of the racing car branch of the business and got designer Gordon Murray to concentrate on the Grand Prix side of the operation. The team had been in the doldrums since the days of its 1967 constructors' title and in 1976 Ecclestone turned to the Alfa Romeo flat-12 engine after a long relationship with Cosworth. Niki Lauda joined the team from Ferrari in 1978 and was involved with the development of the famous 'fan car', the BT46B. After Lauda powered it to victory in the Swedish Grand Prix it was later outlawed

and banned, although the Swedish result was allowed to stand.

Shortly after switching to the V12 Alfa engine Lauda announced his retirement and in 1980, with the brilliant new Brazilian Nelson Piquet in the team, Ecclestone returned to the Cosworth power supply for his BT49. Piquet lifted the world crown in 1981 but Brabham had to content itself with second place in the race for the constructors' crown behind the fast-developing Williams.

In 1982 Brabham switched to the BMW engine but enjoyed only one win, at Montreal. The following year Piquet won his second world title but again the Constructors' Cup eluded the team when this time they came third behind Ferrari and Renault.

The TAG-Porsche-powered McLaren proved too good for the Brabham, and indeed all other teams in 1984 and again in 1985. In 1986 with funds dwindling and their star driver Piquet moved to Williams, Brabham had its worst season since coming into Formula One and collected a mere two championship points. To

make matters worse Gordon Murray quit and moved to McLaren. That was to be the last straw as Brabham went through a dramatic decline in fortunes. Ecclestone kept the team going in 1987 and at Adelaide a pair of BT56s was seen for the last time. Sadly neither car finished the race which summed up Brabham's finale.

Bernie Ecclestone is not finished with Formula One and is still involved via FISA and FOCA. He had just had enough of dipping into his own pocket to finance the team. Towards the end of the 1988 season, Ecclestone sold the entire Brabham shareholding to Walter Brun, boss of the EuroBrun Team.

Whether Brabham return to Formula One or not, because of their excellent record over the years they will never be forgotten. And there are other great, and nostalgic, names of Grand Prix racing that will linger forever. One such name is that of **Mercedes Benz**.

Daimler and Benz have been associated with motor racing since the early days at the turn of the century when manufacturers sought to promote their car. One only has to look at the magnificent road car produced by the German company these days to see that its policy eighty years ago was absolutely right. Gottlieb Daimler first started building internal combustion-engined cars in 1886 and Karl Benz built his first cars around the same time. In 1901 Daimler's cars became known as 'Mercedes' to attract sales in France, and in 1903 at Athy in Northern Ireland a Mercedes won the Gordon Bennett Trophy with Camille Jenatzy behind the wheel, the start of the company's great record in motor sport.

In 1915 Mercedes conquered the United States when they won the Indianapolis 500 and in 1926 Daimler and Benz merged to form the Daimler-Benz company based at Stuttgart. Their cars were subsequently called Mercedes-Benz.

The first great racing cars produced by the new company were the S-type series sports cars. However, Hitler saw Grand Prix racing as a propaganda platform and consequently gave State money to the Daimler-Benz factory to produce the 'best' Grand Prix cars, which is just what the company did. Between the early 1930s and the outbreak of the war the magnificent supercharged silver painted cars dominated the Grand Prix scene. Their only rivals were fellow German manufacturers, Auto Union.

Lella Lombardi made history at the 1974 British Grand Prix when she became the first woman to enter a world championship race. Unfortunately she failed to qualify in her Brabham BT42.

Left: Bernie Ecclestone, the man who took over the Brabham team from Jack Brabham, has done so much for racing, not only with the Brabham team, but as a member of the Formula One Constructors' Association (FOCA).

Right: The Brabham team at the 1987 Australian Grand Prix. It was the last Grand Prix to feature a Brabham before they pulled out of Formula One. Happily, after a year away the famous marque returned in 1989 when Walter Brun bought Bernie Ecclestone's interests in the company.

The first of the great Mercedes Grand Prix cars was the W25 designed by Dr. Hans Nibel. Streamlined, it was long and low, and was well ahead of its time. Its straight-eight 3.36 litre engine was capable of 354bhp. Rival Italian manufacturers Maserati and Alfa Romeo were only producing cars with output in the region of 200bhp.

After a disappointing season in 1936 Mercedes set about producing their next great car, the W125. Regarded as the most powerful Grand Prix car ever built, its 5.6 litre engine gave an output of 646bhp and was capable of speeds of over 200mph (322kph). The W125 was only seen for one season, 1937, but it completely overwhelmed the opposition. A new formula was devised for 1938 restricting supercharged cars to a 3 litre capacity and was obviously designed to curb the German domination. Despite these changes Mercedes produced yet another winner in the W154, powered by a supercharged V12 engine. The new car carried on where the W125

left off and more often-than-not the first three places in the major Grands Prix all bore the name of Mercedes' drivers.

The team manager was Alfred Neubauer and he recruited the best drivers of the day – team-leader Rudolf Caracciola, Hermann Lang, Manfred von Brauchitsch, and the Briton Richard Seaman. Neubauer ran a highly professional team; no longer was it an amateur sport as he made winning the sole priority of everybody at the Stuttgart factory.

When Grand Prix racing returned after the war the Germans were not to be seen, and indeed when the world championship started in 1950 the German manufacturers were absent. Consequently the Italians Alfa Romeo and Ferrari had the first two seasons all to themselves. However, this would all change when Mercedes returned to motor racing in 1952.

Initially Mercedes built highly successful 3 litre, 6-cylinder sports cars and won the 1952 Le Mans (also taking second place) and came

Same car different guise: the revolutionary W196 Mercedes. The streamlined version was the first to appear but was later replaced by the more conventional version.

Next page: Eddie Cheever behind the wheel of the Alfa Romeo during the 1985 German Grand Prix. It was the last season for the famous marque.

second in the Mille Miglia. Mercedes was back! Neubauer was still racing manager and when they returned to Grand Prix racing in 1954 he got the best drivers once more; this time he recruited Juan Manuel Fangio, Karl Kling and Hans Herrmann.

The car that Mercedes returned to Formula One with was the revolutionary W196, the silver grey car that came in two forms: the streamlined sporty looking version or the more conventional racing car with the pointed tail. Both were great cars. Powered by a 2½ litre engine with Bosch fuel injection the W196 was a classic and in 1954 won five races as Fangio became World Champion. It was the same story the following year when Fangio won the title in the slightly modified W196 with new team-mate Stirling Moss taking second place as the Mercedes won five of the six championship races (not including Indianapolis).

Moss also won the Targa Florio and Mille Miglia in the 300 SLR sports car to confirm Mercedes was back among the elite of motor racing. But having come for a second time and conquered for a second time, at the end of 1955 Mercedes announced it was pulling out of racing in the

wake of the Le Mans disaster in which 81 people lost their lives and which involved one of their cars. They have since turned briefly to other forms of racing, and in 1988 made a comeback in sports car racing, but they have never returned to Formula One; if they do, other teams had better beware!

During Mercedes' brief return to Grand Prix racing in the mid-1950s one of the teams who tried to stop their dominance was the Italian **Maserati** company, who had a racing team with an excellent tradition of its own, but who was no match for the German outfit in those two years. They have, however, enjoyed golden days of their own.

The six Maserati brothers started their association with motor racing by making sparking plugs at their Bologna factory in the early 1920s. Two of them, Alfieri and Ernesto were keen drivers and in 1925 made their first car for Diatto. When Diatto pulled out of racing they used the car as the basis for the first to bear the Maserati name and it made its debut in the 1925 Targa Florio.

In 1930 they produced the remarkable Tipo V4 Sedicai Cylindrini which contained two super-

charged 2 litre 8-cylinder engines mounted side-by-side. Difficult to handle because of the strengthened chassis it was, needless to say, very fast! The 3 litre 8CM became a very popular single seater among private entrants after its release in 1933.

Despite producing the very fast 3 litre Tipo 8CTF for the 1938 Grand Prix formula, it was not good enough to beat the Germans. However, the Tipo proved itself in America and won back-to-back Indianapolis 500 races in 1939 and 1940 with Wilbur Shaw behind the wheel on each occasion.

The Maserati brothers retained control of the company until 1938 when they sold to Omer Orsi. In 1948 the brothers eventually left to form the OSCA team and that same year the successful Maserati 4CLT/48 made its debut in the San Remo Grand Prix, taking first and second places.

When the world championship started in 1950 Maserati were no match for the Alfa Romeo team and it was not until 1953 when Fangio won at Monza that a Maserati had its first championship win. After deserting the team for Mercedes, and then Ferrari, Juan Manuel Fangio re-

turned to Maserati in 1957 and won his fifth and final world title in the famous 250F.

One of the classic cars of the post-war era, the 250F was the most successful of the Maserati Grand Prix cars. Neat and compact, the first model in 1954 had a 2½ litre 6-cylinder engine capable of developing 240bhp. By the time Fangio drove the car in 1957 it had been uprated to 260bhp, and now had a five speed gearbox. Today, one of the most popular cars at historic races is the 250F.

In 1957 Maserati at last conquered all opposition, and at the end of the season announced it was quitting Formula One having achieved its goal. However Maserati continued to make great sports cars capable of winning world titles and in 1966 returned to Formula One when the Chipstead Motor Group, their concessionaires in Britain, bought out the Cooper team. They supplied their V12 engine to the team for two years.

Life for any Italian Formula One team these days is not an easy one having to live in the shadow of Ferrari. But at one time the greatest name in Italian motor racing was that of **Alfa Romeo**, who dominated the world

championship in its inaugural year, 1950. But the Alfa story goes back a lot further than that.

Alfa Romeo made its debut, albeit inconspicuously, in the 1919 Targa Florio, and by the end of the 1920s was the most dominant team in sports car racing. Between 1930–35 Alfa won the Targa Florio six years in succession and between 1928 and 1939 they won the Mille Miglia eleven times, including eight in succession from 1932–39. Add to that four consecutive Le Mans wins from 1931–34 and there is no denying Alfa's superiority. Of course, these successes did nothing but good for the sales of their classic road cars which contained the same twin overhead cam engines as their racing counterparts.

In the 1920s and 1930s the sight of the great Nuvolari driving an Alfa was one of the finest in motor racing and in the mid-1930s Alfa proved it was capable of taking on and beating the Germans of Mercedes and Auto Union with their classic single seater, the 2.9 litre Tipo B. And in the 1935 German Grand Prix it had one of its best wins when Nuvolari's Alfa beat the Germans on their own soil. Hitler was not amused and he made sure the situation was soon rectified.

After the war, with the Germans missing from Grand Prix racing, Alfa had the chance to dominate again and they modified their 1938

straight-eight 158 'Alfettas' which were capable of producing 335bhp. They recruited top drivers Farina, Fagioli and Fangio and in the inaugural world championship season won all the six races they entered. The following season they won four of the seven European Championship rounds as Fangio became the team's second world champion after Farina. But towards the end of the season their domination began to slip as Ferrari became the leading manufacturer. To remain competitive Alfa needed more money and they turned to the Government for help. They refused and Alfa Romeo temporarily ended its long association with Grand Prix racing.

Alfa had been supplying engines to the Brabham team since 1976 but in 1978 they made the decision to return with their own car and at the Belgian Grand Prix the Alfa Romeo Tipo 177 brought back one of the great names into the world championship. Sadly, the 'new' Alfa could not add to the team's tally of world championship wins from the 1950s and after the 1985 season they quit once more but continued to supply their V8 turbo engine to other teams.

In 1949 British Racing Motors, better known as **BRM**, was formed with the intention of showing the world that British engineering was still capable of competing with the best. The company was set up by Raymond Mays who

Left: Tazio Nuvolari in the 2600cc Alfa Romeo in 1933.

Right: The BRM V-16 with Juan Manuel Fangio behind the wheel in 1952 . . . one of the few occasions Fangio drove a BRM.

wanted to 'sell' the car to the racing fans of Britain by way of a co-operative, but it didn't work and in 1953 after a series of disasters – and completely against his basic principle of the team being run by a wealthy individual – Mays was forced to sell to Sir Alfred Owen of the massive Rubery Owen Organization.

The first BRM looked good and underneath its bonnet the V16 supercharged engine promised so much. However, on its debut in the *Daily Express* Trophy at Silverstone in 1950 transmission problems saw the car left on the start line. At Silverstone the following year the two BRMs of Reg Parnell and Peter Walker made a surprise appearance at the British Grand Prix. They fared well, finishing 5th and 7th, but after another appearance at Monza they stayed out of Grand Prix racing over the next four years.

BRM returned to Formula One in 1956 and in 1959 they did, at last, enjoy their first Grand Prix success when Jo Bonnier won at Zandvoort. That was the first of 17 wins over the next thirteen years.

Having switched from their own engine to the Coventry-Climax unit in 1961, they continued with a programme of advancement in 1962 after new team manager and chief engineer Tony Rudd had been told: 'win two Grands Prix or the team folds'. Graham Hill piloted the car to four

championship wins which gave him the world drivers' title and BRM the constructors' title. The team was saved thanks to Rudd's work on their own V8 1497cc engine which powered the P57.

Despite the reliability of the car and Hill's expertise they could not win another world title because of the presence of Ferrari and Lotus. In 1969 BRM lost the services of its saviour, Tony Rudd, who teamed-up with rivals Lotus. BRM reached its lowest ebb since its early days in Formula One. With the Tony Southgate designed P160 they made a temporary recovery in 1971 but thereafter it was a downward slide and in 1974 the Owen Organization withdrew its support and it brought about the end of Raymond Mays' dream. For three more years BRM continued under the Stanley-BRM banner after Sir Alfred Owen's sister, Jean Stanley, came to its rescue with financial aid, but the final demise came in 1977.

While BRM was expected to be the first British team to gain world championship glory, Tony Vandervell crept in and gained that distinction with his **Vanwall** marque in 1958. Ironically, Vandervell, who had been building cars since 1932, was one of the first manufacturers to support Raymond Mays' BRM project, but he later withdrew his support to develop his own Formula One car.

Above: John Surtees in the BRM P139 during the 1969 British Grand Prix at Silverstone.

Right: The Honda V12 at the 1968 Spanish Grand Prix.

The proprietor of VP Bearings, Vandervell's first car was the 'Thinwall Special' named after the company's Thinwall bearing. It was a 4½ litre Ferrari and was launched in 1954. This formed the basis for his first Vanwall which derived its name from his own surname and that of the Thinwall.

The inaugural Vanwall was built around the Ferrari chassis and with a concocted Norton engine; Vandervell was a director of the Norton Motor Cycle company at the time. The car made its debut in the BRDC Trophy at Silverstone in June 1954 but mechanical problems soon put it out of the race. Teething problems continued in 1955 and the following year Vandervell completely redesigned the car. A five speed gearbox was fitted and a new 4-cylinder engine, designed by Colin Chapman of Lotus, was installed into the space-frame chassis. Frank Costin designed the new sleek body. Vanwall was nearly ready to conquer the world.

With Stirling Moss behind the wheel the new Vanwall won the 1956 International Trophy at Silverstone and the following year Moss and Tony Brooks steered the car to a shared victory in the British Grand Prix at Aintree, the first British Grand Prix win for thirty years. Moss followed that with wins at Pescara and Monza. The

following season Moss and Brooks steered the car to six Grand Prix wins to win the inaugural Constructors' Championship for Tony Vandervell. Sadly 1958 was to be Vandervell's swansong. Ill-health forced him to retire and with it his team quit Formula One.

With Vanwall out of Grand Prix racing it didn't mean the end of the British challenge. Fortunately the Colin Chapman and John Cooper teams were up-and-coming and ready to take over the Vanwall mantle. And it was **Cooper** who took the constructors' title from Vanwall in 1959.

John Cooper first took an interest in motor racing when his father built a 500cc motor cycle powered car for him in 1946. Revolutionary because the engine was mounted behind the driver, these cars attracted a lot of interest and John and his father were soon asked to make similar cars for other enthusiasts of Formula Three. Suddenly this revolutionary car became very popular and it led to the formation of the Cooper Car Company. The first cars, which are the forerunners of the modern-day Grand Prix car, used a 500cc JAP speedway engine. Cooper then switched to the more powerful 499cc Manx Norton motor cycle engine.

In the early 1950s the company turned its attention to front engined Cooper-Bristol Formula Two cars and also to MG- and Jaguar-powered sports cars, but wanted to develop a mid-engined Formula One car. They tried their successful Formula Two car (a bigger version of their original Formula Three prototype) in a couple of Formula One races in 1957. The 1.5 litre Climax powered car performed well, but was not powerful enough to match its Formula One counterparts.

In 1958 the rear-engined revolution was really under way, and the Cooper T45 with the larger Climax engine won the opening two rounds of the world championship. As we have seen, Vanwall recovered to take the title, but Cooper was very much a team to watch and had to be taken seriously as title contenders.

With the full 2½ litre Climax engine in 1959, and the great Australian Jack Brabham behind the wheel, the Cooper team was to enjoy its first great season when Brabham won the drivers' title and Cooper the Constructors' Cup. Both titles were retained in 1960 as the T51 and T53 won six championship rounds. Brabham retained his title while team-mate Bruce McLaren was runner-up.

But as often happens, the innovator is often eclipsed and having been the first successfully to race mid- or rear-engined cars, other teams soon followed suit and were producing more

competitive cars. Cooper had a minor revival in 1966 when John Surtees won the final race of the season in the new Maserati-powered Cooper, but John Cooper no longer controlled the company. Following a bad car accident he was forced to sell to the Chipstead Motor Group, the British concessionaires for Maserati, hence the new power unit in the T81 in 1966. Despite this mini-revival, the company was on its last legs and in 1968 the second great British Formula One team pulled out of Grand Prix racing.

Cooper certainly left its mark on Formula One, and the same can be said of both Honda and Renault. Japanese motor cycle manufacturer **Honda** came into the four-wheeled branch of motor sport with an excellent pedigree behind them, but only for two wheels. However, Honda boss Soichiro Honda had a dream of dominating car racing in the same way as his company had with bike racing. He set off in pursuit of that dream in 1964 when his first car made its debut in the German Grand Prix.

A sleek looking car, it was powered by a 1945cc V12 engine capable of producing 210bhp, and that was about all it produced in its debut season. The following year the much improved RA272 won the last race of the season in Mexico City with Richie Ginther behind the wheel. It was the last race under the old 1500cc formula.

With the launch of the new formula the following year Honda started to fall behind the other leading manufacturers. The season was nearly four months old before their new car, the RA273, appeared but it was too late to make any impact. John Surtees joined the team in 1967 and he enjoyed a surprise win at Monza in the new Eric Broadley-designed RA300 which was to be the team's second and last Grand Prix win. That same year they pulled out of motor cycle racing and in 1968, after a troubled year with their cars, they left Formula One as well.

Honda returned to bike racing in 1979 and after a spell providing engines for Formula Two and Formula Three cars, they returned to Formula One in 1983 as suppliers of engines to the Frank Williams team. Their turbo power unit has since become one of the most efficient and reliable in the business and powered the team to the constructors' title in 1986 and 1987. A year later, after switching their allegiance to the McLaren team, their engines proved invincible as they enjoyed a share of the Constructors' Cup for the third successive year.

When **Renault** launched their turbo-charged RS01 in 1977 there were those who thought it a mere gimmick and indeed, when the turbo-

Left: The Renault staff with their last Grand Prix car in 1985.

Right: Renault revolutionized Grand Prix racing in 1977 when they launched their turbo-charged engine unit.

charger was responsible for Jean-Pierre Jabouille's retirement on lap 17 of the British Grand Prix at Silverstone, the pundits had good cause to mock. But, ten years later, every Formula One team had used a turbo-charged engine to power their cars.

Renault's arrival in Formula One in 1977 followed the appointment of former sports car driver Gerard Larrousse as the director of Renault Racing the previous year. But Renault was not new to motor racing, they were around in the early days of the great city-to-city races at the turn of the century.

In the 1970s Renault had supplied power units for the Alpine sports cars and also provided a very successful unit for Formula Two cars. But it was in Formula One that Renault was to make its biggest and most lasting impression. Renault brought about a resurgence of power to Grand Prix racing, and after winning their first race at Dijon in 1979 the rest of the motor racing world had to take notice. But furthermore, the motoring world in general followed the French company's lead and most production cars have turbo-powered units in their top-of-the-range models.

Renault's first turbo engine was a twin overhead cam 1492cc V6 design which was capable of producing 510bhp at 11,000rpm. After a couple more years of development and testing, its output was increased to a massive 1300bhp. Because of the increase in power over the next ten years the sport's governing body announced in 1986 that turbos were being phased out completely by the start of the 1989 season. But even though turbos have now gone, the contribution of Renault to Grand Prix racing will never be forgotten.

Renault stopped producing their own car in 1985 after the TAG, Honda and BMW units became more competitive than their own, but continued making units for Lotus, Ligier, and Tyrrell in 1986. However, they discontinued supplying units in 1987 and 1988 but returned in 1989 as suppliers of the new 3.5 litre V10 unit designed by Bernard Dudot for the Frank Williams team.

Many teams have come and gone; they have all had dreams like those of Renault, Lotus, Cooper, BRM, and some have been lucky enough to fulfil those dreams while others have not. But all the teams who have competed in Formula One have one thing in common, they have enjoyed the thrill of competing in the world of Grand Prix racing and at the same time have thrilled the fans.

73

3. Sponsorship

Sponsorship is a necessity of modern-day sport. Most sports would struggle to survive without it and motor racing is no exception, especially as the cost of the development and production of the finely tuned Formula One cars has spiralled in recent years. Grand Prix racing has been described as the world's richest circus as it travels across the continents from circuit to circuit each season and that description can't be denied in a sport that talks in seven-figure salaries for its leading performers.

Because of its nature and the high cost of its basic equipment, motor racing has always been an expensive sport to engage in. Even in the early days of Formula One a figure of £10,000 was required to put a couple of cars on the road – and keep them there.

In 1970 Ken Tyrrell's total Formula One budget was £80,000. Today, it is in the region of £10 million to keep one car for a season. McLaren need around £4½ million for the salaries of Alain Prost and Ayrton Senna, and that is before they start paying the other salaries and for the cost of engines and other components. Engines alone cost in the region of £40,000 each.

Even in the 1930s when it was the enthusiastic amateur who kept motor racing alive, he still needed a healthy bank balance in order to pursue his 'hobby' as a little bit of financial help from a local garage was about all he could hope for in those days.

Things changed before the Second World War when Grand Prix racing was used as a platform for national pride, and German and Italian propaganda. These countries invested large sums of money in their respective motor car industries; however, when Alfa Romeo pulled out of Grand Prix racing in 1951 it was the end of an era. Alfa was the last team to receive state subsidy. From now on, motor racing had to be self-sufficient. But who pays for it all? The sponsors, of course. Yet, it is not a one-way arrangement; sponsors get their fair share of the spoils by the way of advertising.

There is some prize money in motor racing. It is calculated using various factors; starting position, race position at the quarter-, half-, and three-quarter stage, plus an accrued system based on the team's standing in the world championship. But prize money of around £100,000 for a race will knock only a small dent in a team's £10 million budget.

Motor racing is a great spectator sport and the sixteen-race programme will be watched by more than one million fans each year. That is on race day only; practice sessions attract large crowds as well. But the big 'prize' for the sponsors is television coverage.

Grand Prix racing is televised either live, or shortly after each race, to more than fifty countries. That means a viewing audience of nearly 1,500 million, which averages 90 million per

Left: The cars may not have been plastered with sponsors' names in 1935 but sponsors were prepared to pay to have their products advertised around the circuits of the day as this picture from the Swiss Grand Prix at Bremgarten shows.

Right: Sponsors' names as far as the eye can see ...

Previous page: Sparks flying from the *John Player Special* Lotus, one of the best known names in Grand Prix racing since the start of big sponsorship involvement.

race. World-wide, those figures represent the equivalent of nearly fifty *days'* Grand Prix coverage per year. Because of that, advertising in motor racing can be regarded as cheap and it is easy to understand why multi-national companies are particularly keen to invest in motor racing.

In the early days of championship racing many teams relied on a fee for merely appearing on the starting grid and prize money was the main source of income for some teams as they sought to break-even at best. In the 1950s, wealthy drivers often paid for the privilege of driving racing cars – another form of income. Sponsorship did, of course, exist but only in a small way, and more by way of subsidy rather than as a commercial venture. There has always been a selection of advertising hoardings around the tracks. But since the age of television, almost every piece of the circuit which catches the 'eye' of the camera carries a hoarding advertising one product or another.

It has been a different story in the United States for some time. The great Indy cars relied upon sponsorship and it became a big-money sport much earlier with sponsors being rewarded for their investment by seeing their company name and logo plastered over the great Offenhausers, and other racing vehicles they supported.

As financial aid became more crucial in the 1950s and '60s, help came from the oil, tyre and engine manufacturers; all motor industry allied industries. But in 1968 the ever innovative Colin Chapman started the boom which led to the current trend in motor racing sponsorship. He attracted an outside sponsor and part of the deal was to have his familiar green Lotus painted in the company's brand colours.

With the CSI relaxing its restrictions on advertising on cars, Chapman was the first to take advantage. His first 'clients' were the John Player tobacco company who had the red and gold livery of their *Gold Leaf* brand daubed over the Lotus 49.

Chapman had little difficulty in attracting sponsors. After all, he had a championship-winning car and, in Jim Clark, the sponsors were to have the best driver in the world powering their 'brand name' around the world's great motor racing circuits.

Sadly for Chapman, Lotus and the sponsors, Clark was to lose his life shortly after the deal with John Player when he was killed at Hockenheim in April 1968. But the invasion had started and sponsorship from companies outside the motor trade started coming into the sport. Long gone were the days when cars were painted in the traditional national colours, and the only name to appear on the car was that of the driver and/or manufacturer. Suddenly sponsors' logos were starting to fill the body until, today, there

Above left: The car that started it all, the *Gold Leaf* Lotus 49 in 1968.

Above right: Hospitality tents are a main feature at most major sporting events these days. Motor racing is no different as sponsors use the occasion to entertain business clients.

Right: It is not only the cars and drivers who carry the sponsors' names, but the mechanics as well.

Left: Some Grand Prix races are sponsored. The *Toyota* car company sponsored the 1982 Long Beach Grand Prix, won by Niki Lauda who received this splendid trophy.

WINNER

**TOYOTA GRAND PRIX
OF
LONG BEACH**

1982

Below: Frog's legs, l'Escargot, a bottle of *Moët* and the Monaco Grand Prix . . . what more could a person ask for?

is very little of a car that is not utilized as a mobile advertising hoarding.

Following John Player's lead, other non-allied companies such as Yardley Cosmetics came into Grand Prix racing, and when the floodgates opened there was no limit to the companies prepared to lend their name to a Formula One car; even the London Rubber Company had their *Durex* brand of contraceptive plastered over the Surtees car. And when Player's wanted to promote their new cigarette brand, *John Player Special* they had the Lotus cars painted in the familiar black and gold colours. The team even became known as John Player Lotus.

One of the sport's best sponsorship deals was signed in 1974 when Philip Morris cigarettes signed a deal with the McLaren team to have their cars painted in the red and white colours of their *Marlboro* brand. Fourteen years later McLaren still carry the name on their cars. The *Marlboro* name has been closely associated with motor sport for many years on both sides of the Atlantic, and before teaming up with McLaren, sponsored the BRM Formula One team for two years.

Soon, cars became identifiable by their sponsor's colours as much as for their distinctive

designs and millions of watching eyes would have little problem in picking out the John Player Lotus or Marlboro McLaren. And that is, after all, what advertising is all about; getting the product over to as many people as possible, and as easily as possible . . . even if it is not the cheapest way of doing it!

Firms like Bang and Olufsen, Hitachi, Matchbox, First National City Bank and Embassy soon joined the ever-increasing list of sponsors. Bang and Olufsen, John Player and others were not content with being involved in sponsoring just a team, they also sponsored Grand Prix races following the lead of the International Wool Secretariat who sponsored the 1971 British Grand Prix which incorporated the *Woolmark* name in the title.

Today, many of the world championship races are sponsored. A look at the list of the 1988 races and their sponsors gives an indication as to which companies are prepared to invest between £250–500,000 in a Grand Prix, and also shows how diverse the companies involved in Formula One are: British GP: *Shell Oils*/Italian GP: *Coca-Cola*/Portuguese GP: *SG Gigante*/ Spanish GP: *Tio Pepe*/Japanese GP: *Fuji Television*/Australian GP: *Foster's Lager*. But does it all work?

Well, the cost is certainly favourable, especially when compared with the cost of a thirty-second television advert. But, of course, advertising is an unknown quantity. It is also a necessity of modern-day society. No matter what the merits of advertising, one company who can claim to have reaped the benefits of being involved with Formula One is the Italian knitwear manufacturer Benetton. Since they came into the sport as sponsors of the Tyrrell team in 1983 the company has enjoyed a period of growth.

They are now a much respected Formula One team in their own right. Furthermore, sales of their products have soared. Five years ago, very few people had heard of Benetton goods. Now, their shops can be found in most major towns. So the answer is . . . yes, motor racing sponsorship does work. Benetton did come into the sport with more than just a sponsorship deal, they formed their own team, but the end product has been the same: sales have gone up. To have achieved equal world-wide awareness of their product by other forms of advertising would have cost them more than their investment in their own Formula One team.

But the Grand Prix circus is used beyond its television appeal. Companies utilize the spectacle of the Grand Prix as a means of entertaining business clients and such circuits as Silverstone, Paul Ricard, Adelaide, and so on, can be seen

Above: The Benetton livery has certainly added plenty of colour to the world of Formula One.

Right: Gerhard Berger in the 1986 Benetton. A year later he was driving the familiar red marque of Ferrari.

Left: Hardly a piece of Nigel Mansell's overall is unused as sponsors scramble to have their name embroidered onto his clothing . . . at a cost, of course.

littered with hundreds of hospitality tents on race days as one client attempts to lure business from another with the aid of champagne, smoked salmon and Grand Prix racing as a backdrop.

There are plenty of companies prepared to come into Formula One racing but the financial package has got to be right for the team as well as for the sponsors. The best deals are the long-term ones. A team like Williams, whose main sponsor is the office equipment company Canon, former sponsors of the Football League, have a turnover of around £12½ million per annum. They have a staff of around one hundred, and four of them are constantly on the telephone speaking to potential sponsors. Williams have been lucky because they have had an eleven-year deal with fuel suppliers Mobil. But to show how delicate such deals are, it is worth looking at Williams' engine problems of the last couple of seasons.

Williams fell out with Honda in 1987 after four very successful years. Mobil supplied fuel to the team. In 1988 Williams turned to a new engine supplier, Judd. Again Mobil provided the fuel. Then, in 1989, Williams turned to the normally-aspirated Renault engine. No problems, until you realize Renault have a tie-up with French fuel suppliers Elf, a connection Mobil will not accept too lightly. So what next? The team's success centres around a competitive engine but it also needs Mobil's cash which, sadly, will not be forthcoming in 1989 following the deal with Renault. But will a big sponsor continue to plough money into a team that is not winning? And how much does it all cost in terms of hard cash? Mobil, for example, paid £1.2 million to have a sticker on either side of the two Williams cars. That sort of money is not easy to replace, hence the dilemma over the Renault deal.

Main sponsors, like Canon, pay in the region of £2 million per year, while other Williams' sponsors like ICI will pay £1.5 million to have a sticker on one of the Williams cars. Barclay cigarettes pay a 'mere' £1 million.

The *Denim* brand name of cosmetics was introduced into motor racing in 1983 because they felt the image of the racing driver nicely fitted the image of their own products. For the privilege of having a logo on Nigel Mansell's overalls in 1987 they paid Williams £750,000. But the pick of Mansell's apparel went to engine sup-

pliers Honda, who supplied more than £3 million worth of engines, and contributed another £3.4 million towards the retainers of the two drivers, Nigel Mansell and Nelson Piquet. It all seems a far cry from 1960 when Innes Ireland was paid a mere £500 as a retainer by Esso to become Team Lotus's number one driver, although on top of that he collected a third share of all start money and £1-a-mile for a race win. Victory could give him in the region of £1,500 but out of his income he had to pay his own expenses . . .

Cigarette companies have used motor racing as an advertising medium since 1968. Today, many of the leading teams have tobacco companies as main sponsors. McLaren, as we have seen, are sponsored by *Marlboro*, who also are the principal joint sponsors (with Agip petroleum) of the Ferrari team. Lotus are sponsored by *Camel*, the brand name of the R.J. Reynolds cigarette company who are keen to oust *Marlboro* as the world's number one cigarette. Another cigarette company, the French-made *Gitanes*, are the main sponsors of the Ligier team, and tobacco company *West* are Zakspeed's main sponsors.

Other non-motor industry companies who acted as leading sponsors of 1988 Formula One teams were: *Canon* cameras and office equipment (Williams); financiers *USF&G* (Arrows); and the clothing firms *Lois*, *Courtaulds* and *Benetton* who are the main backers of Minardi, Tyrrell and Benetton's own team.

Money is such an essential factor in Grand Prix racing that it can even assure a driver of a ride if he can bring cash into the sport. Satoru Nakajima got his chance to drive with the Lotus team because it was part of the deal that went with Honda's agreement to supply engines to the English team, while Adrian Campos's £1 million worth of sponsorship that he brought with him to the Minardi team in 1987 was influential in his acceptance on the team.

Motor racing is the most expensive sport in the world and cars go through money as fast as they go through petrol. The commercial manager is just as important a part of the modern day racing team as the designer and chief engineer. It is pointless developing the most efficient car in the world if you cannot afford to get it into production: the only thing that can do that is money.

Left: Cigarette companies have used motor racing as a powerful source of advertising. *Camel*, for example, lend their name to the Lotus team.

. . . The End!

4. Past Champions

Motor racing has never followed the Olympic belief that taking part is more important than winning. It has thrived on the desire to win and drivers have always wanted to go faster than rivals. The Grand Prix driver in the early days of racing had the same desire as his modern-day counterparts, even though his lifestyle was so very different. There were no such things as Swiss tax havens for the top drivers, and the notion of arriving at meetings in private jets and helicopters was a far cry from the Grand Prix driver of 1988. But the successful driver then was held in the same esteem as the likes of Prost, Piquet, Senna and Mansell in the eighties.

Before Grand Prix racing started in 1906 the sport had the first of its heroes in **Leon Thery**, a Frenchman who won the last two Gordon Bennett races.

Born in 1878 he was a competent mechanic. Known as 'The Chronometer' he drove in the Paris–Bordeaux race at the age of 21. He then powered his Richard-Brasier to victory at Taunus in 1904 to lift the Gordon Bennett trophy, thus bringing the trophy back to France for the first time since 1901. He became the first, and only, man to win the trophy twice when he beat the Italian FIATs of Nazzaro and Cagno at Auvergne a year later to establish the French car industry as the best in the world once more.

Surprisingly, when the first French Grand Prix was held at Le Mans the following year, Thery was not among the leading contenders. Naturally, being the instigators of the first Grand Prix, the French wanted to maintain their standing of the Gordon Bennett days and indeed it was a Renault which won the first race in 1906, but with a Hungarian driver, Ferenc Sziz. But then the French domination ended. The Italian Fiat won the 1907 race and in 1908 Mercedes transferred the prestige to the Germans. Thery was not alive when the French emerged triumphant again in 1912; he died from tuberculosis at the age of 29 in 1909.

French pride was restored when **Georges Boillot** won the revived French Grand Prix at Dieppe in 1912 in a French-made Peugeot. Something of a hero already, Boillot was a candidate for canonization when he was crowned French Grand Prix winner for a second time in 1913, again driving a Peugeot. Those two successes were the only major ones of his career but he did enough to restore national pride to the French motor car industry. His brother Andre won the 1919 Targa Florio in a Peugeot.

As the Great War approached, the last French Grand Prix before the hostilities was at Lyons in 1914. It was an ideal chance for the French to gain a psychological advantage over the Germans before true 'battle' commenced. But sadly, the French were devastated when Mercedes filled the first three places despite a brilliant drive by Boillot. It was Boillot's last race – he was killed when shot down over the Western Front in 1916.

The German charge at Lyons was led by **Christian Lautenschlager**, the first of the great German drivers.

Lautenschlager's career may have been fairly uneventful after the 1914 French Grand Prix, but that day at Lyons he not only demonstrated his own personal skill, but showed the world what a powerful nation Germany had become in the motor car industry. Forty years later they were still producing great racing cars. Today they are producers of quality road cars.

Born into poverty in 1877 Lautenschlager spent his early years working in Switzerland before getting a job at the Daimler factory (later Mercedes). He then became a works Mercedes driver and enjoyed his first major win in the 1908 French Grand Prix at Dieppe. After the war he curtailed his Grand Prix activities, but raced in the Targa Florio and Indianapolis 500.

Previous page: Clark waiting patiently at the start of the 1967 German Grand Prix at the Nurburgring.

Right: Tazio Nuvolari (driving) and co-driver Compagnoni during the 1933 Mille Miglia which they won in their Alfa Romeo.

Left: Louis Chiron (No. 40) during the 1947 Swiss Grand Prix at Bremgarten.

Below: Louis Chiron in his Talbot before the start of the 1948 British Grand Prix at Silverstone, the first ever Grand Prix held over the famous Northamptonshire circuit.

Inter-War Years

Louis Chiron's career spanned 28 years and in the 1920s his duels with Tazio Nuvolari were legendary. Born in Monte Carlo, he won Monaco's two principal races; the Monaco Grand Prix (in 1931) and the Monte Carlo Rally, at the age of 55 in 1954. Having passed his driving test at the age of 13, a career in driving looked a certainty, and during military service at 17, he was employed as a chauffeur to various French Marshals. After earlier success in a privately entered Bugatti, in 1923 Chiron joined the Bugatti works team. One of his greatest races was the 1931 Monaco Grand Prix when he won by over three minutes and set the lap record in the process.

After an eight year retirement he returned to racing in 1945 and won the 1947 French Grand Prix in a Lago-Talbot. When the world championship was launched in 1950 'The Wily Old Fox' was nearly 51 years of age but between then and 1955 he took part in fifteen races. When he started the 1955 Monaco Grand Prix he was 55 years 292 days old at the time. He remains the oldest man to start a world championship Grand Prix. He died in June 1979.

The 'Golden Arrow' in which Sir Henry Segrave recaptured the world land speed record for Britain at Daytona in 1929. He clocked a speed of 231.21mph (372.08kph).

Bryan De Grineau

Between 1926 and the outbreak of the war **Rudolf Caracciola**, better known as 'Caratsch', was one of the most outstanding drivers of this time and can rightly claim to be among the greats of the sport. A consistent driver and regular winner, Caracciola was a master tactician and never pushed a car beyond its limit. His skill rendered the hammering of the throttle an unnecessary evil.

Contrary to his apparent Italian name, 'Caratsch' was born in Germany, at Remagen on the Rhine. After proving himself as a hill-climber he was offered a place in the successful Mercedes team and in 1926 won his first Grand Prix, the inaugural German Grand Prix at Avus. Over the next thirteen years he won the race another five times.

When Mercedes pulled out of racing in 1931 he joined the Italian Alfa Romeo team, and enjoyed continued success. While practising for the 1933 Monaco Grand Prix however, a bad accident hospitalized him for a year. By the time he had recovered, Mercedes were back in racing, and 'Caratsch' was back on the team.

After the war he became a naturalized Swiss and retired from racing in 1952, although he never competed in the newly instituted world championship. A failing liver brought about his death in 1959 at the age of 58.

For a man whose popularity in Italy ranked just below that of the Pope, there can be no doubting **Tazio Nuvolari**'s place among the pantheon of motor racing. Many regarded 'The Flying Mantuan' as the finest driver of them all, including the late Enzo Ferrari. Standing at just over five-feet tall, Nuvolari was constantly seen wearing a grubby yellow shirt beneath which lay an ice cool man with enormous courage and determination.

He started his career racing motor cycles but turned his attention to cars full time in 1929. He joined the Alfa Romeo team and his first major success for them was in the 1930 Mille Miglia, a race he was to win a second time in 1933.

During the 1930s he was invincible, winning all major Grands Prix, as well as other major races like Le Mans (in 1933) and the Targa Florio in 1931 and 1932.

Fed up with the politics at Alfa he formed his own team with Baconin Borzacchini in 1934 and for two years they raced 3 litre Maseratis and 2.6 litre Alfas.

In 1935 Nuvolari was ordered by Mussolini to rejoin the Alfa team as the country's motor industry was being threatened by the Germans, and the country's top team needed its star performer back among its ranks. But his skill alone was not good enough for a team that was being

overtaken by the superior German Auto Unions and Mercedes. By 1938, Alfa had lost interest in racing and Nuvolari was free to leave and join the Auto Union team.

After the war he won the Albi Grand Prix in a Maserati but by now his health was failing and in 1953 he died at the age of 61. As stipulated, he was buried wearing his familiar grubby yellow shirt.

One of the great British drivers of the 1920s and '30s when men like Nuvolari and Caracciola were dominant, was **Sir Henry Segrave**. Fearless, Segrave was not only a master of the great circuits like Brooklands, but he was to set world land and water speed records.

Educated at Eton, Henry O'Neal de Hane Segrave served in the Royal Flying Corps during the First World War but was shot down on his last mission. While recovering he started driving an Opel, and that was the start of his love affair with racing. His ambition to join the Sunbeam Racing Team was fulfilled in 1921 when they gave him a car for the French Grand Prix on the understanding he pay for any damage! Segrave didn't win, but he didn't do any damage to the car, and he was invited to join the team on a regular basis. Britain had never secured a victory in Grand Prix racing but the Sunbeam was capable of rectifying that situation and Segrave the man capable of pushing the car to the chequered flag for the first time. Segrave adopted a

Above left: 'Caratsch' (nearest to camera) in a 1927 Mercedes.

Above centre: Rudi Caracciola enjoyed a few years racing after the war before his retirement in 1952. He is seen here in his Mercedes, just about to be overtaken by the man on the bike!

Above right: The rugged and diminutive Tazio Nuvolari, described by many as the greatest of all time.

Right: A man of adventure and high speed, Henry Segrave, setter of world records on land and water.

Next page: Juan Manuel Fangio made a nostalgic return to the Grand Prix arena at Rio de Janeiro in 1987.

policy of starting races slowly, but finishing rapidly, and in 1923 this tactic paid off as the team had its first success winning the French Grand Prix at Tours.

In 1926 Segrave became the fastest man on earth when he took an aero-engined Sunbeam to 152.33mph (245.099kph) along Southport sands. The following year he retired from motor racing to concentrate on pushing up the land speed record, which he did, taking it beyond the 200mph (517kph) mark.

In 1930 he also set a world water speed record but a few months later was killed when his boat hit a log on Lake Windermere. Segrave was only 34 at the time, but in his short life he had become the fastest man in the world on land and water, and had helped establish Britain in the world of Grand Prix motor racing.

Post-War Years

The post-war years have, of course, been dominated by world championship Grand Prix racing. The following, with the one exception of Stirling Moss, have all won the world drivers' championship, and are no longer racing in Formula One.

Turin-born Doctor **Giuseppe Farina** holds a special place in Grand Prix racing history as the sport's first world champion. He was 44 years of age when he won the inaugural title in his Alfa Romeo 158 and 159 in 1950. Apart from winning the first world title, he holds the distinction of winning the first championship race, at Silverstone, on 13 May 1950. That was one of three wins in his championship year.

By the time the championship arrived Farina,

known as 'Nino', had been involved in racing for seventeen years, starting as a hill-climber in 1933. Enzo Ferrari noticed the talent of this man who showed great courage and determination, and signed him for his Scuderia Ferrari team which raced Alfas. In 1938 he joined the Alfa works team and drove a 158 to his first major victory, the 1940 Tripoli Grand Prix.

Despite remaining with Alfa after the war he announced his retirement in 1946 but in 1948 returned and was seen driving a Maserati. His 'retirement' followed a dispute with the Alfa bosses, but their differences were patched up and he rejoined the team for the start of the first world championship season. Then, when Alfa pulled out of Grand Prix racing in 1951, Farina teamed up with Ferrari once more, but had to play second fiddle to Ascari.

Farina escaped serious injury during the 1953 Argentine Grand Prix when he skidded into the crowd after trying to avoid a spectator on the track. Fifteen people were killed, but Farina suffered only a sprained ankle.

The following year he was involved in another bad accident in the Mille Miglia from which he never recovered, and in 1955 Farina announced his second retirement. While on his way to watch the 1966 French Grand Prix at Rheims he was killed in a car accident in the French Alps.

Argentina's **Juan Manuel Fangio** is often accredited as being the greatest post-war driver. Others, like Jim Clark, can rightly challenge Fangio for that 'title' but if one considers Fangio's record in the world championship alone, then his claim must be taken seriously. He won the title a record five times, and his twenty-four

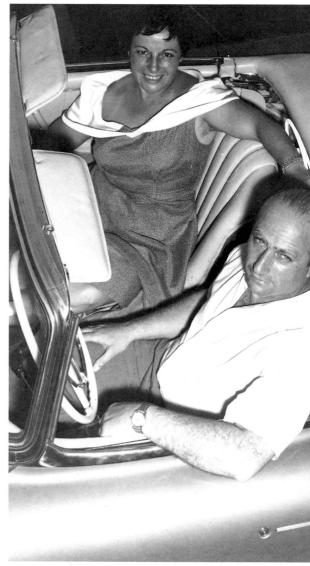

Grand Prix wins set a record that stood until surpassed by Jim Clark in 1968. Fangio was 39 when the world championship was launched in 1950 and 46 when he won his fifth title.

Born in 1911 he started his racing career as a travelling mechanic when he was 17 but did not start driving seriously until 1933 when he used to drive Model 'A' Fords and Chevrolets in his home country. He first came to Europe in 1948 and his famous blue and yellow Maserati soon became a familiar sight. Sadly the car did not match up to Fangio's apparent skill. When Alfa Romeo returned to racing, they recruited the Argentinian to their team for the first world championship but he could only finish runner-up to the first champion, Farina.

The following year Fangio won his first world crown but when Alfa pulled out of racing he returned to Maserati. However, a bad accident at Monza forced him to miss most of the 1952 season. Back with a vengeance in 1953 he finished second to Ascari, but in 1954 won the first of four consecutive world titles first for Mercedes then the new Lancia-Ferrari team and then, eventually, for Maserati.

After the 1958 French Grand Prix he announced his retirement after fifty-one world championship races.

During the Formula Two world championship years of 1952 and 1953 **Alberto Ascari** and his Ferrari 500 were unbeatable. They won 11 of the 15 championship rounds (Indianapolis excluded) and swept to two consecutive titles.

Ascari started racing motor cycles at first, but turned to cars in 1947, initially with Maserati.

Top left: Giuseppe Farina after winning the 1950 British Grand Prix, the first ever world championship race.

Top centre: Juan Manuel Fangio shortly after a great win in the 1953 Italian Grand Prix when he snatched victory on the last lap.

Top right: Fangio in the Maserati 250F on his way to the 22nd Grand Prix win of his career at Monaco in 1957.

Left: Fangio after his retirement in 1958. He is seen here on holiday with his wife.

Above right: Three great Italians: Gigi Villoresi (left), Enzo Ferrari (centre) and Alberto Ascari, who was the 1952 and 1953 world champion, and the first champion in a Ferrari.

Right: Ascari on his way to winning the 1953 Dutch Grand Prix in the Ferrari 500. It was one of five wins that season that helped him retain his world title.

He had his first major success in the 1949 Argentine Grand Prix when he beat his mentor, Luigi Villoresi into second place. Shortly afterwards the pair teamed up at Ferrari. Ascari had his first world championship success in the 1951 German Grand Prix at Nurburgring. In 1952/53 he won a record nine consecutive championship races.

In 1954 Ascari was lured by the new Lancia team, but had to wait until the end of the season for his first car. The following year during the Monaco Grand Prix he escaped with his life when his car plunged into the harbour. Ascari swam to safety with nothing more than a broken nose. But four days later, while testing the new Ferrari Sport 3000 at Monza, he lost his life. Thirty years earlier his father had also lost his life on the track when driving an Alfa Romeo at Montlhery.

Britain's **Stirling Moss** must surely be the best driver never to have won the world title. Four times runner-up, in successive years 1955–58, he had to live in the shadow of the great Fangio and then Mike Hawthorn.

He made his debut just after the war in a hill-climb at Stanmer Park, Brighton, England. When he graduated into the senior ranks of racing he insisted on driving British cars; a decision which surely cost him a world title.

In his early days he drove Jaguars in sports car races and competed in the Monte Carlo Rally. He had his first world championship race in the 1951 Swiss Grand Prix behind the wheel of an HWM. After three seasons, and driving for a succession of British manufacturers, ERA, Connaught and Cooper-Alta, Moss had still not registered a win, although he had shown his obvious skill in mastering his vehicle, even if the vehicle was often not up to the task.

Just before Mercedes returned to racing in 1954 he offered his services to team boss Alfred Neubauer, who insisted he proved he could win before he considered the Englishman for the German team. Moss went out and acquired an Italian Maserati. He won the Gold Trophy race at Oulton Park, the *Daily Telegraph* Trophy and finished a creditable third in the Belgian Grand Prix. Neubauer was impressed and in 1955 Moss was recruited as the second Mercedes driver to Fangio. The two men filled first and second places in the 1955 world championship and Moss registered his first win in the British Grand Prix at Aintree. He also did his new team proud by winning the Mille Miglia and Targa Florio in 1955 proving himself a great all-round driver.

Moss joined Maserati in 1956 when Mercedes pulled out of racing, and again was second in the championship to Fangio, who was now with Lancia-Ferrari. It was the same story in 1957; Fangio 1st, Moss 2nd. This time Moss had teamed up with the new British Vanwall team led by Tony Vandervell. He drove the Rob Walker privately entered Cooper-Climax in 1958 and, with Fangio retired, Moss was widely tipped as the champion elect, but fellow Briton Mike Hawthorn pipped him to the title by one point, despite Hawthorn's one Grand Prix win to Moss's four.

Right: Stirling Moss, unquestionably the finest British driver never to have won the world title.

Left: Stirling Moss giving advice to Mike Hawthorn before a race in 1958 . . . perhaps he shouldn't have done: Hawthorn pipped Moss to that year's world title by one point.

Moss was never to get that close to the title again. Third for the next three years his career came to an abrupt end at Goodwood on Easter Monday 1962 following an accident which nearly claimed his life. Realizing he would never be as competitive again, Moss made no attempt to make a Formula One comeback and retired.

As popular as ever, the first of the great post-war British drivers is still very much involved in the sport as a journalist, and in recent years he has been seen taking part in saloon car and historic sports car races.

Unlike his contemporary Stirling Moss, who was a dedicated professional, **Mike Hawthorn** was the last of the great amateurs in the mould of the 1930s drivers.

Hawthorn made an impact at Goodwood in 1952 when, within the space of a few hours, he won two races and was second in another in a Formula Two Cooper-Bristol. After half a dozen more Formula Two successes he was invited to test at the Ferrari factory, and the legendary team boss Enzo Ferrari had no hesitation in offering the Briton a place on his team. Like Moss, Hawthorn was patriotic and reluctantly teamed up with Ferrari because of the lack of competitive British cars.

Hawthorn made his Ferrari debut in the 1953 Argentine Grand Prix at Buenos Aires. Six months later he became the first Briton to win a championship race when he beat Fangio in a classic duel to take the chequered flag in the French Grand Prix.

Fourth in the championship that year, he improved to third in 1954 but after a traumatic year, in which his father was killed in an accident, Hawthorn left Ferrari to join the new Vanwall team. However, their cars were not quite ready for an assault on the Formula One world championship and Hawthorn failed to get among the points. His season was not one of total failure because he won the Le Mans 24 Hour Race in a 'D' Type Jaguar with Ivor Bueb. Sadly, the victory was not one of celebration, because it was the race in which more than 80 spectators were killed in the sport's most horrific tragedy.

Hawthorn returned to Ferrari in 1957 and, despite his failure to register a win, finished fourth in the drivers' championship. The following year the Briton was champion when he beat Moss by a mere point. However, Hawthorn, like the rest of the motor racing world, was saddened by the death of his Ferrari team-mate

Far left: Stirling Moss getting into a Maserati before a testing session at Modena in 1959.

Left: Despite a bad accident which nearly killed him in 1962, Stirling Moss maintained a close contact with the sport. He is seen here lending his experience as a broadcaster.

Right: Stirling Moss receiving a trophy from President Peron of Argentina.

Below: Mike Hawthorn leads the field in his Ferrari during the 1958 Italian Grand Prix. He is followed by two Vanwall drivers, Stirling Moss and Stuart Lewis-Evans but it was Tony Brooks, another member of the Vanwall team, who took the chequered flag.

Peter Collins. The tragedy so affected Hawthorn he left racing at the end of the season.

Three months later Mike Hawthorn lost his life when his 3.4 Jaguar crashed and hit a tree on a public road.

The son of a Sydney greengrocer, **Jack Brabham** was the Australian Midget Cars champion five times between 1947–51. After racing Coopers in his home country, he came to Britain in 1955 and competed in the British Grand Prix at Aintree. Sadly, his car was not capable of living with the Mercedes of Moss and Fangio.

Brabham knew that if he was to become a top driver he had to return to Europe and in 1957 he was back. He joined the Cooper Grand Prix team and was to be a leading member as their revolutionary rear-engined car made an attack on the world championship.

Brabham, a master behind the wheel, was also a skilful engineer and the team was doubly to benefit from his experience as it became one of the sport's top Grand Prix outfits.

His first Grand Prix success was in the 1959 Monaco Grand Prix and that season he went on to win the drivers' championship and Cooper the constructors' title, a success they both repeated a year later.

At the end of 1961 Brabham left Cooper to concentrate on developing his own car. With the help of fellow Australian and top designer Ron Tauranac, the first car was ready in 1962. In 1966 Brabham was world champion for a third time. Early in the season he was awarded the OBE for his services to motor racing.

Brabham retired from racing in 1970 after 126 Grand Prix starts and 14 wins. His three sons, Geoff, Gary and David are now following in his footsteps and are showing the same skills as their illustrious father. Geoff is shining on the US circuit while Gary is showing outstanding form in Formula Three and is only a 'stone's throw' away from graduating to Formula One.

In winning the world drivers' title in 1961 **Phil Hill** became the first North American to win the title. He remained the only driver from his country to win the title until Mario Andretti lifted the crown in 1978.

Born at Santa Monica, California in 1927, Hill was a quiet and reserved man. He was little known at the time of his world title, and did little after his world championship success. But he had served his 'apprenticeship' and enjoyed a great deal of success in the world of sports cars having driven for the Ferrari sports car team since 1955.

After winning the 1958 Le Mans, Enzo Ferrari elevated Hill to his Formula One team as number two driver to Mike Hawthorn, after the team lost both Luigi Musso and Peter Collins earlier in the year. Hill played his part in helping Hawthorn lift the title.

Hill enjoyed his first win in the 1960 Italian Grand Prix at Monza and the following year Ferrari were among the most competitive of teams following the introduction of the new 1½ litre formula. Driving the Dino 156, Hill won at Spa and Monza to clinch the championship by one point from team-mate Wolfgang von Trips who was killed in the penultimate race of the season at Monza.

That was to be the American's swansong. He never enjoyed any further Formula One glory as his 1962 Ferrari was not competitive, nor were the Italian ATS and British Cooper he subsequently drove. He still dovetailed his Formula One career with sports car racing and won Le Mans on two more occasions, in 1961 and 1962, before concentrating full-time on sports cars. He eventually retired in 1967.

Graham Hill was the second British world champion. Ironically, like the first, Mike Hawthorn, he was tragically to lose his life away from the danger of the race track.

After twenty-two years of racing, most of it in Formula One, Hill retired in 1975 to develop his

own racing team. Before the year was out Hill, promising young driver Tony Brise, and other members of his Embassy team were wiped out when the Piper Aztec, piloted by Hill, crashed on to Arkley golf course near Elstree, on its return from France.

Born in London in 1929 Hill started life as a mechanic and got a job with Colin Chapman at Lotus. When they went into Formula One in 1958 Hill talked his way into the team. Graham's obvious talent was soon spotted and he was invited to join BRM in 1960. Two years later in their V8 P57 he won his first Grand Prix in the opening race of the 1962 season at Zandvoort. He added three more races to his tally as he ended the season as champion, 12 points ahead of Jim Clark.

, Runner-up to fellow Britons Clark (twice) and John Surtees in the three years 1963–65, Hill returned to Lotus in 1967. In the meantime he had earned himself a reputation as one of the most colourful characters on the circuit. Furthermore, he had shown his versatility in 1966 by winning the Indianapolis 500 in a Lola-Ford. He was also becoming something of a Monaco expert as he won the famous race through the streets of Monte Carlo no less than five times.

Left: Two great names from the past, Australia's Jack Brabham (left) and Britain's Stirling Moss.

Right: Australian Jack Brabham with his Cooper-Climax in 1958.

Below: The familiar helmet of Graham Hill, twice world champion in 1962 and 1968.

A second world championship followed in 1968 when he won by eight points from Jackie Stewart. Hill received a bad injury at the end of 1969 and his competitive edge went after that, despite winning the 1972 Le Mans with Henri Pescarolo. However, he was determined to revive his competitive spirit with his new Embassy team, but sadly, that November day in 1975 put paid to this dream.

His son Damon has shown signs of possessing dad's skills and has enjoyed wins in the British Formula Three championship.

Scotland's **Jim Clark** epitomized all that is great about motor racing. He was unquestionably one of the greatest drivers of all time. But off the track the quiet man was the perfect advert for the sport. Dedicated, he was the complete professional.

Born in Fife in 1936 the son of a sheep farmer, his first motoring exploits were in his father's Austin Seven around the farm. He made his racing debut in a DKW saloon in 1956. Two years later he met Colin Chapman and that was to be the start of one of the best relationships in motor sport. With Chapman's innovative skills, and Clark's talent, Lotus and Jim Clark were to conquer the world of Formula One.

Clark made his Grand Prix debut at Zandvoort in 1960; two years later he enjoyed the first of his twenty-five wins when he took the chequered flag at Spa. In 1963 Clark was crowned world champion after winning a record seven championship rounds. Not surprising, the Coventry-Climax powered Lotus 25 helped Chapman's team to the constructors' title. It was another double for Clark and Chapman in 1965 as the Scot powered his way to his second title 14 points clear of his nearest rival, Graham Hill. Clark showed his superiority that season by taking on the Americans in their own backyard and became the first overseas winner of the Indianapolis 500.

Clark spent his entire Formula One career at Lotus and in 72 Grands Prix occupied pole position no less than 33 times. He was only intent on winning, second place was not good enough for Clark. He was only once second in those 72 races.

The motor racing world was deprived of its greatest talent in April 1968 when his car careered off the Hockenheim track in West Germany during a Formula Two race. Today, twenty years later, Jim Clark is still remembered, and still regarded as the greatest of all time.

John Surtees has a special place in motor sport history; he is the only man to have won world titles on two and four wheels.

Having won seven world motor cycling titles at 350 and 500cc he turned his attention to the four-wheeled branch of motor sport. His dedication and determination was to carry him to another world title.

He started his career as a sidecar passenger for his father at the age of 15 in 1949. Surtees won the first of his world titles in 1956 when he took the 500cc title on an MV Agusta.

He started car racing in 1960 and, when his bike commitments permitted, drove for the Lotus Formula One team. The following year he concentrated on cars full time with the Cooper team. In 1962 he drove the Lola Mk. 4 before being invited to join the Ferrari team in 1963. That year he had his first Grand Prix win, at the Nurburgring.

As the 1964 championship came to its last race, in Mexico City, Surtees was in with a chance of the title, but trailed Graham Hill by 5 points. Surtees finished second and Hill was out of the points so the title went to Surtees by a single point. In contention for his second title in 1966 he quit Ferrari mid-season following a dispute and moved to Cooper. He ended the season runner-up to Jack Brabham.

After that he moved to Honda in 1967, and to

Left: Jim Clark in the famous green Lotus 49 at Silverstone.

Right: The tartan headband means it can be only one man, Scotland's three times world champion, John Young 'Jackie' Stewart.

Below left: John Surtees with his Formula Two Cooper, with which he made the transition from bike racing to car racing in 1960.

BRM in 1969. In 1970 and 1971 he raced his own Surtees-Ford, but with no success. In fact, in the eight years between 1970–78 his cars started 118 races but failed to register a win. Surtees himself won six races from his 111 starts during his driving career.

New Zealander **Denny Hulme** won a scholarship to Europe in 1960. With the sports car and Formula Two experience gained in his home country, he was given a drive with the Formula Two Coopers.

In 1961 he joined Jack Brabham's staff as a mechanic and at the Brands Hatch Boxing Day meeting he won the Formula Junior race in a Brabham – the first ever victory for any Brabham car. In 1965 he had a couple of drives in the team's Formula One car.

Hulme succeeded Dan Gurney as the Brabham number two driver in 1966. The following year the New Zealander won his first Grand Prix, at Monaco, and went on to beat his 'boss' into second place in the world championship. He quit Brabham at the end of his championship year and joined fellow New Zealander Bruce McLaren's new Formula One team.

Having driven for McLaren's in Can-Am races in 1967, he returned to North America in 1968 to win the Can-Am series. He regained the title in 1970 and his 22 wins is an all-time Can-Am record.

Although a consistent performer in Formula One, Hulme never came close to winning the world title a second time and at Buenos Aires in

1974 he had the eighth and last of his Grand Prix wins. He retired at the end of that season and returned to New Zealand with his family.

Friendly and affable, Hulme was the man who helped the McLaren team through its troubled times after the shock death of Bruce McLaren in 1970.

Scotland's remarkable tradition of producing world champions continued after Jim Clark's death with the arrival of Dumbarton's **Jackie Stewart** on to the Formula One scene.

Stewart followed his brother Jimmy into motor racing, and had his first race at Oulton Park in a Porsche in 1962. In 1964 he teamed up with the man who was to become a great friend and partner during his glory days, Ken Tyrrell.

Tyrrell signed Stewart for his Formula Three team, and they enjoyed their first win at Snetterton. The natural progression to Formula Two was also in a Tyrrell car and in 1965 BRM recruited the Scot for their Formula One team to be replacement for Richie Ginther as Graham Hill's number two. Stewart's first season in Formula One produced a victory at Monza and he finished the season third in the championship, just behind Jim Clark and team-mate Hill.

After winning the opening race of 1966 at Monte Carlo Stewart's progress was hindered following a bad crash at Spa. He returned from the shadows in 1968 when he teamed up with his mentor Tyrrell once more who was now in Formula One with the newly formed Matra team. Stewart took the new car to second place in the drivers' championship and the following year he won the first of his three world titles, helping Matra clinch the constructors' title.

Tyrrell ran the new March team in 1970 but their car was not good enough for Stewart who had developed into one of the great drivers of the modern era, and before the 1970 season was out Tyrrell started work on a Formula One car of his own. By 1971 the Tyrrell 001 was ready, and was good enough to help Stewart to his second world title. Two years later Stewart won five championship rounds on his way to his third title.

Having started in 99 Grands Prix and won a record 27, which stood unchallenged until surpassed by Alain Prost in 1987, Stewart announced his retirement shortly after the death of his team-mate Francois Cevert during practice for the 1973 United States Grand Prix at Watkins Glen. Many teams tried to tempt Stewart back to racing, but even the largest of cheques have proved to be no incentive for him to return to the sport.

An expert clay-pigeon shooter, and close friend of the Royal Family, Stewart is still involved with motor racing as a television broadcaster and interviewer.

Although regarded as the first Austrian world

Left: Chapman and Clark were the famous Lotus duo. At Tyrrell it was Ken Tyrrell (right). and Jackie Stewart.

Right: One of Jochen Rindt's early successes. He is seen holding aloft the London Trophy after winning the Formula Two race at Crystal Palace in 1964 when he beat Jim Clark and Graham Hill into 2nd and 3rd places.

Below: Jackie Stewart was not only an excellent racing driver, he was a dab hand at clay pigeon shooting.

champion, **Jochen Rindt** was in fact born in Germany, in 1942. His parents were killed when he was only a year old and he was brought up by his Austrian grandparents.

Rindt first started racing saloon cars in 1962. Within two years he exploded through the ranks to Formula One and made his debut in a Brabham-BMW at Zeltweg. He got a regular drive in the Rob Walker Cooper in 1965, but the machinery did not match up to Rindt's apparent skill, which he displayed in that year's 1965 Le Mans when Rindt and Masten Gregory won the famous race in a privately entered Ferrari 250LM.

Despite his great skill, Rindt all too often piloted inferior machinery. This was certainly the case at Cooper and also at Brabham whom he joined in 1968. It was the same story in his first season with Lotus in 1969, although the Lotus 49 provided him with his first Grand Prix success at Watkins Glen.

In 1970, at long last, things started to go right for the Austrian in the new Lotus 72. He won five of the first eight championship races, including four in succession. But, race number ten was to be the last for the likeable champion-elect. A very fast but safe driver, Rindt inexplicably swerved into a guardrail during practice at

Monza at almost the same spot where Wolfgang von Trips was killed nine years earlier. Rindt was dead before his arrival at hospital. He led the world championship by 20 points from Jack Brabham at the time of his fatality. At the end of the season his points total was good enough to give him the championship posthumously, the only time this has ever happened.

Since 1970 Brazil has produced three great Formula One drivers: Nelson Piquet and Ayrton Senna are current stars, but their first world champion was **Emerson Fittipaldi**. The son of a motor racing journalist, Fittipaldi was the 1965 Brazilian Karting champion. Two years later he was Formula Vee champion in a car produced with the help of his brother Wilson.

Fittipaldi came to Europe to race in Formula Ford in 1969 and his wins led to his promotion to Formula Three. The following year he was racing Formula Two and the fairytale continued when, in May 1970, Colin Chapman gave him a Formula One drive in the old Lotus 49 in the British Grand Prix; Fittipaldi finished 8th from the back row of the grid. Then, after only three Formula One drives, the Brazilian found himself team leader after Jochen Rindt's tragic death and at Watkins Glen in 1970 he won his first Grand Prix.

Two years later he swept all aside as he won five races on his way to his first championship in the Lotus 72. Only 25 at the time, Fittipaldi remains the youngest winner of the world crown. He had another season at Lotus, finishing runner-up in the championship to Jackie Stewart, before joining McLaren in 1974, and in the M23 he powered his way to his second world title.

Runner-up in the 1975 championship, this was to be the end of Fittipaldi's great reign. He joined his brother's Copersucar team in 1976 but the car was not competitive enough and in 1980 Emerson stopped driving.

Fittipaldi invested his money in a 200,000-tree orange plantation in Brazil, and bought a minor interest in the Hugo Boss fashion empire. He is now enjoying a revived motor racing career on the American Indy Car circuit.

For sheer bravery, the exploits of Austrian **Niki Lauda** in 1976 have been unsurpassed in recent Grand Prix racing. Thirty-five points clear of Britain's James Hunt, Lauda was on course for his second successive world title with seven races remaining when disaster struck at the Nurburgring, a circuit Lauda had publicly condemned as unsafe.

On the second lap his car hit a kerb, flew out of control and burst into flames. Lauda was dragged out; his life was saved, but he was to be

Above: The first of the great Brazilian drivers, Emerson Fittipaldi, world champion in 1972 and 1974.

Right: Niki Lauda, world champion three times, twice after his horrific accident at the Nurburgring in 1976.

scarred for life. Six weeks after being given the last rites he was back behind the wheel of his Ferrari determined to hold on to his world title, but at the end of a dramatic season, Hunt edged him out by one point.

The son of a paper-mill owner, Lauda was born in 1949 and started racing Mini Coopers in 1968. Three years later he had his first Formula One drive in a March 711 at the Austrian Grand Prix. The John Player Formula Two champion in 1972, he joined the BRM Formula One team in 1973. Despite having an unsuitable car, Lauda gave some impressive drives attracting the attention of Enzo Ferrari whose team he joined in 1974.

His first Grand Prix win was in the Ferrari 312 at Jarama in his first season with the Italians. It was the first of 25 wins in a Grand Prix career which lasted fourteen years. The following year Ferrari and Lauda reigned supreme as he won five races on his way to his first world title. Had his accident not intervened in 1976 he would surely have retained that title. But as it was, he got it back in 1977.

Lauda moved to Brabham in 1978 but after two seasons announced his retirement to con-

centrate on his airline business. However after two years away from the limelight he was tempted back by McLaren and in 1984 he was world champion for a third time when he beat teammate Alain Prost by the narrowest of margins (half a point) to clinch the title.

After 171 Grand Prix starts Lauda announced his second retirement in 1985. And this time he has stuck to his word.

James Hunt was Britain's last world champion, but how different the story might have been had Niki Lauda not suffered those horrific burns at the Nurburgring.

Hunt started racing a Mini 850 in 1967 and soon graduated to Formula Three from Formula Ford. But it was during his latter career that he was involved in several accidents that earned him the nickname 'Hunt the Shunt'. A series of disasters for the one-time 'hot-head' of racing led to his temporary obscurity. But then came along Lord Hesketh, a man similar in temperament to Hunt. Hesketh gave Hunt Formula One drives in a March before introducing his own car, the Hesketh 308 during the 1974 season.

Hunt was, by now, showing signs of being a good driver. Long gone were the heady days of

Formula Three, and at the 1975 Dutch Grand Prix at Zandvoort he steered the Hesketh to the first win for driver and car. When Emerson Fittipaldi left McLaren in 1976 Hunt was offered the team-leader's job. By now he had developed into a mature driver, and it showed as he lifted the world title for Britain.

Hunt stayed with McLaren for two more seasons but felt the new ground-effect cars were taking some of the skill away from the drivers. He had a final season with the Wolf team in 1979, but retired before the season was out. Fully aware of the dangers of racing he decided to quit and began a new career as a commentator. Between 1973–79 Hunt started in 92 races, and won 10, all in the three seasons 1975–77.

Although **Mario Andretti** is regarded as the second American winner of the drivers' championship he was, as his name implies, born in Italy. He lived in Pisa and used to watch in awe as the Mille Miglia passed through the town each year. In 1955, when Andretti and his twin brother Aldo were teenagers, the family emigrated to the United States.

Mario's love of racing started when he watched the 1954 Italian Grand Prix. He took up stock

Left: James Hunt in the McLaren M26 (1978).

Right: After many years of perseverance South Africa's Jody Scheckter eventually won the world title in 1979, but that was to be his swansong.

car racing and then midget car racing on his arrival in the States. He started racing single seaters in 1964 and was three times the USAC champion. But he was determined to get into Formula One, despite making a lot of money from single-seater racing in the USA.

Colin Chapman gave him his first chance when he offered him one of his cars for the 1968 US Grand Prix at Watkins Glen. Andretti surprised everybody by powering his way to the front of the grid, with Jackie Stewart alongside him. He further surprised the near 100,000 crowd by pulling away from Stewart on the opening lap and built up a two-second lead. But Andretti had to pull out of the race with clutch problems on lap 33. He had three races for Lotus in 1969 but it was at Indianapolis that he enjoyed his greatest moment winning the famous '500' in record time.

Andretti joined the March Formula One team in 1970 and in 1971, with Ferrari, he had his first Grand Prix win at Kyalami. But Andretti was still dovetailing his Formula One and Indy-Car careers. After two and a half seasons driving Formula One for the unsuccessful Parnelli team he re-joined Lotus in the latter half of 1976 and

four Grand Prix wins in 1977 pushed him to third place in the championship. The following year the Lotus pair of Andretti and Ronnie Peterson dominated the championship with Andretti taking the title.

After a couple more seasons in Formula One, first struggling with Lotus and then with Alfa Romeo, Andretti returned to his beloved Indy Car racing. He is still winning races in the United States where one of his keenest rivals is his son Mike.

Born at East London, South Africa, the one-time home of the South African Grand Prix, **Jody Scheckter** started racing Karts at the age of 11. He progressed from there and brought his skills to Europe in 1971 when he was aged 21. The following season he was in the McLaren Formula Two team and, at Watkins Glen in the final Grand Prix of the season, he made his first Formula One appearance.

He did not have his first win until the 1974 Swedish Grand Prix after he teamed up with Ken Tyrrell and was driving the Cosworth-powered Tyrrell 007. That year he was a title contender but finished third behind Emerson Fittipaldi and Clay Regazzoni.

In 1976 Scheckter had the honour of steering the Tyrrell Project 34 six-wheeler to its first Grand Prix success at Anderstorp. And after finishing third in that year's world championship the South African joined the new Wolf Engineering team and in the opening race of the 1977 championship he won the Argentine Grand Prix to make Wolf the first manufacturer since Mercedes in 1954 to win on its world championship debut.

Sadly, the car struggled in 1978 and for the new season Scheckter was behind the wheel of the more competitive Ferrari 312. He won three championship races, as did Ferrari team-mate Gilles Villeneuve. At the end of the season they filled first and second places in the championship with Scheckter taking the top spot.

Scheckter's championship season was followed by one of disaster due to a substandard car and at the end of the 1979 season Scheckter retired at the age of 30. A very talented driver,

Scheckter competed in 112 races and was in the points in no fewer than 53 of them; 10 of them being first places.

Alan Jones's rise through the ranks of Formula Three, Formula Atlantic and Formula 5000 was not an easy one. Hard work and dedication took Jones to the pinnacle of his career in 1980.

Born in Melbourne in 1946 Jones started racing in the early 1970s and got his Formula One break in 1975 when he raced a privately entered Hesketh. But his sponsor withdrew and it looked like the end for the likeable Australian until he got a slot in the Graham Hill team, albeit temporarily, for the remainder of the season.

Jones got a job with the Surtees team in 1976 and, despite the car not being impressive, Jones *did* impress and the following season he teamed up with Shadow as a replacement for Tom Pryce who lost his life in the third race of the 1977 season. Driving brilliantly, Jones won the Austrian Grand Prix in the rain and mist at the

Previous page: The 1980 world champion Alan Jones made a second comeback in 1986 with Lola.

Right: One of the sport's great showmen, Keke Rosberg of Finland, the 1982 world champion.

Far right: Rosberg in a Williams, in which he won his world title.

Osterreichring, and announced to the world that he was a future world champion.

He joined Williams in 1978 and after a season of consolidation the following year he showed that he was the man to beat. However, despite winning four races (more than any other driver) he could only finish third in the championship. But the next season held glory for Jones and the Frank Williams team as they lifted the drivers' and constructors' titles.

Jones announced his retirement at the end of the 1981 season, despite still being one of the top drivers on the circuit. He returned to his native Australia to run a cattle farm. But, like former champion Niki Lauda, the retirement was short-lived, and he made a return in 1983 when he answered Jackie Oliver's call to help out the Arrows team in the Long Beach Grand Prix, just two months after Jones broke a leg in a fall from his horse. Jones enjoyed a second 'comeback' with the Lola team in 1986.

Like former world champions Mario Andretti and Jochen Rindt, **Keke Rosberg** was not born in the country he represented at the time of lifting the world title. Rosberg was born in Sweden in 1948, but was a naturalized Finn.

A great showman, Rosberg was the winner of the Scandinavian and Finnish Kart titles in 1971, and he went on to win the Formula Vee titles in 1973. He had his first Formula One drive with Theodore in the 1978 South African Grand Prix and his first win in the 1982 Swiss Grand Prix driving a Williams. In between he drove for Wolf and Fittipaldi. That one win helped him to the world title by five points from Britain's John Watson and France's Didier Pironi.

Rosberg stayed with Williams three more seasons, and won four more races. Although consistent, he was never competitive enough to challenge for the world title again and after one season with McLaren in 1986 he retired after 114 races.

5. Today's Drivers

Formula One driving for fun disappeared in the late 1950s when it became a highly competitive sport. Even so, drivers of twenty-five years ago could never have imagined the lavish lifestyle that would be bestowed upon their counterparts a quarter of a century later. Understandably, in a sport that is so dangerous, 'danger money' has to be paid, and today's top Formula One drivers are among the highest paid of all sportsmen.

Thanks to sponsorship, Alain Prost, Nelson Piquet, Ayrton Senna and Nigel Mansell all command seven figure salaries, and all nearer £2 million than £1 million. Evidence of the rewards are the lavish luxury homes often in tax havens. Nigel Mansell, for example, lives on the Isle of Man, while Alain Prost lives in Switzerland.

For further proof that motor racing is highly paid, the driver of today arrives at a race meeting in either his private jet or helicopter. At the 1960 British Grand Prix at Silverstone, Innes Ireland, Jack Brabham and Colin Chapman all had the 'audacity' to fly to the meeting in a private plane and were reprimanded by the race secretary. Twenty-one years later at the corresponding race more than 1,500 aircraft movements were recorded during the meeting. Today, often before the last drop of champagne is drained from the Jeroboam, the Grand Prix driver is on

his way back to his tax exile. The rewards are certainly very high, but then again, so are the risks.

The following is a list of all 1988 Grand Prix drivers, their career records, and potted biographies. Records are correct as at the end of the 1988 season:

Michele Alboreto

Born: 23 December 1956, Milan, Italy
Lives: Monaco
Formula One Teams: 1981–83 Tyrrell; 1984–88 Ferrari
Starts: 121
First Grand Prix: 1981 San Marino GP
First Points: 1982 Brazilian GP (6th)
Wins: (5)   1982 Las Vegas GP; 1983 Detroit GP; 1984 Belgian GP; 1985 Canadian GP; German GP
Best World Championship Position: 2nd   1985

One of the many Italians currently in Formula One, Michele Alboreto came to the top flight of motor racing in 1981 after a successful Formula Three career which saw him win the European title in 1980. After joining the Tyrrell team, he dovetailed his activities with the Lancia sports car team and enjoyed considerable success, win-

ning four races with Riccardo Patrese and Piercarlo Ghinzani.

His first Grand Prix win was at Las Vegas in 1982 and before his move to Ferrari in 1984 he had another success to his credit, again in the United States, this time at Detroit.

After a year settling in with his new team, Michele came close to winning the world title in 1985 when he finished second to Alain Prost. Problems in the latter half of the season cost him dearly.

In 1988 the only challenge to the McLaren supremacy was offered by the Ferrari pair of Alboreto and Berger, but they could only finish a poor third and fourth in the championship.

Philippe Alliot

Born: 27 July 1954, France
Lives: Nr. Paris, France
Formula One Teams: 1984–85 RAM; 1986 Ligier;
   1987–88 Lola
Starts: 64
First Grand Prix: 1984 Brazilian GP
First Points: 1986 Mexico GP (6th)
Wins: (0)
Best Finish: 6th   1986 Mexican GP; 1987 German
   GP, Spanish GP, Mexican GP
Best World Championship Position: Jt. 16th   1987

Third in the 1981 European Formula Three championship, and third in the 1983 Le Mans 24 Hour race (with the American father and son pair of Mario and Michael Andretti). Frenchman Philippe Alliot had his first Formula One race in 1984 when he drove for the RAM team in the Brazilian Grand Prix at Rio.

He spent another year with the uncompetitive RAM outfit before spending a year with Ligier and then for the last two years, with Lola. He has the talent, as he displayed in the Spa Formula 3000 race in 1986, but he appears to have been let down by unreliable cars since coming into Formula One.

Alliot is still looking for his first Grand Prix win, and in 1989 is hoping to improve on his best finish of 6th place, which he has achieved four times.

Rene Arnoux

Born: 4 July 1948, Pontcharra, Grenoble, France
Lives: London, England
Formula One Teams: 1978 Martini/Surtees; 1979–
   82 Renault; 1983–85 Ferrari; 1986–88 Ligier
Starts: 140
First Grand Prix: 1978 Belgian GP (Martini)
First Points: 1979 French GP (3rd)
Wins: (7)   1980 Brazilian GP; South African GP;

Previous page: Rene Arnoux in the Ferrari (left) and Eddie Cheever in the Renault, getting to grips with each other during the 1983 European Grand Prix at Brands Hatch.

Left: What price would you put on all that talent?

Right: Rene Arnoux of France, currently the oldest man in Formula One.

Above: Gerhard Berger played a significant role in turning Benetton into one of the leading Formula One teams. Sadly for the team he took his services to Ferrari in 1987.

Right: Gerhard Berger aboard the Arrows in 1985.

Left: Thierry Boutsen in the colourful Benetton in 1988.

1982 French GP; Italian GP; 1983 Canadian
GP; German GP; Dutch GP
Best World Championship Position: 3rd   1983

Currently the oldest driver in Formula One, 40-year-old Rene Arnoux has been competing at the highest level since 1978 when he joined the Martini team.

He had the right pedigree for Formula One, and arrived as the reigning European Formula Two champion. After moving to Surtees in the second half of his first season, he joined the new Renault turbo-powered team in 1979, and it was with them that he enjoyed his first win at Rio in 1980.

The best season of his career was in 1983, his first with Ferrari, when he won three championship races and was only two points behind Alain Prost with two races remaining. But Arnoux failed to pick up anymore points and had to be content with third place behind Prost and the surprise champion Nelson Piquet.

Sacked by Ferrari early in 1985, and replaced by Stefan Johansson, Arnoux returned to Formula One the following season with Ligier. With a point to prove, he finished fourth at Rio and Brands and ended the season with a commendable 14 points. Since then however, he has struggled to find the form that so nearly brought him the world crown in 1983.

Julian Bailey

Born: 9 October 1961, England
Lives: Hertfordshire, England
Formula One Teams: 1988 Tyrrell
Starts: 6
First Grand Prix: 1988 San Marino GP
First Points: None yet
Wins: (0)
Best Finish: 9th   1988 Detroit GP
Best World Championship Position: Never
   classified

A publican from Hertfordshire, Julian Bailey came through the ranks of British racing before being given his Formula One opportunity with Ken Tyrrell's normally-aspirated team in 1988, making his debut at San Marino.

A Formula Ford driver at the age of 17, he progressed through Formula Ford and Formula Three before getting into Formula 3000 in 1987. He gave a great display at Brands where he powered his Lola to victory. The win attracted the eye of Ken Tyrrell, and the following season Bailey was in his Formula One team. 'Julio' still has to make his mark in the top formula, but 1989 could be the season with all teams competing on level terms once more, a change that can only be good for Bailey and Tyrrell.

Gerhard Berger

Born: 27 August 1959, Vienna, Austria
Lives: Kundl, nr. Innsbruck, Austria
Formula One Teams: 1984 ATS; 1985 Arrows;
   1986 Benetton; 1987–88 Ferrari
Starts: 68
First Grand Prix: 1984 Austrian GP
First Points: 1985 South African GP (5th)
Wins: (4)   1986 Mexican GP; 1987 Japanese GP;
   Australian GP; 1988 Italian GP
Best World Championship Position: 3rd   1988

Austrian Gerhard Berger exploded on to the Formula One scene with ATS in 1984. Still racing Formula Three at the time, he soon displayed his potential in Grand Prix racing. Often he gave the impression he was reckless and on the verge of crashing, but always managed to get out of trouble thanks to his obvious skill.

His driving resembles that of another great Austrian, Jochen Rindt. He is fast, but safe at the same time. Having been with three different teams in three years, Berger was snapped up by Ferrari in 1987 after making a favourable impression in 1986, particularly by winning the Mexican Grand Prix in his BMW-powered Benetton.

The great talent of the Austrian showed through in his first season with Ferrari. He won the final two championship races in Japan and Australia to haul himself into 5th place in the championship above team leader Michele Alboreto. In 1988 he improved on his championship position and in the 12th race of the season became the first driver to break the Prost/ Senna domination when he won the Italian Grand Prix at Imola.

Thierry Boutsen

Born: 13 July 1957, Brussels, Belgium
Lives: Monaco
Formula One Teams: 1983–86 Arrows; 1987–88
   Benetton
Starts: 89
First Grand Prix: 1983 Belgian GP
First Points: 1984 San Marino GP (6th)
Wins: (0)
Best Finish 2nd   1985 San Marino GP
Best World Championship Position: 4th   1988

Belgian Thierry Boutsen showed his true worth in 1988, his second season with Benetton. Although he has still to improve on his best finish, 2nd at San Marino in 1985, he was a regular among the points as he outshone his team-mate, Nannini.

Runner-up to Michele Alboreto in the 1980 European Formula Three championship, Boutsen showed outstanding form in Formula Two before joining the Arrows' Formula One team in 1983. He had four seasons with them before joining Benetton in 1987.

Boutsen also starred on the sports car scene and won two world championship races one at Monza in 1983 with Bob Wollek and the other at Spa in 1986, with Frank Jelinski. The Belgian is undoubtedly talented and given the right car is a potential champion. A move to Williams in 1989 as replacement for Nigel Mansell might just realize his potential.

Martin Brundle

Born: 1 June 1959, King's Lynn, England
Lives: Gayton, nr. King's Lynn
Formula One Teams: 1984–86 Tyrrell; 1987 Zakspeed; 1988 Williams
Starts: 55
First Grand Prix: 1984 Brazilian GP
First Points: 1986 Brazilian GP (5th)
Wins: (0)
Best Finish: 4th 1986 Australian GP (was 2nd at Detroit in 1984 but later disqualified)
Best World Championship Position: 11th 1986

Winner of the coveted Grovewood Award in 1982, Martin Brundle finished second to the dominant Ayrton Senna in the British Formula Three championship the following year.

Belgian Thierry Boutsen. After two years with Benetton he replaced Nigel Mansell in the Williams team in 1989.

After a year with West-Zakspeed, Britain's Martin Brundle became one of the 'reserves' at Williams in 1988, but it was in the world of sports cars that Brundle excelled that year when he won the world title.

Ken Tyrrell, as ever encouraging British drivers, signed Brundle for his Formula One team in 1984. He had a dream start, finishing fifth on the opening round of the season at Rio, and three months later, at Detroit, he was second to Nelson Piquet. On the day, Brundle overcame an aching neck and shoulder to drive brilliantly as he took the non-turbocharged car round the tight streets of the American city. Sadly his efforts were wiped from the record books because his car was later found to be illegal, and so his great drives went without the credit they deserved.

Brundle stayed with Tyrrell three seasons before joining Zakspeed in 1987 and in 1988 became one of the 'reserves' in the Williams team. He was called up for duty in the Belgian Grand Prix when Nigel Mansell was sidelined following a bout of chickenpox. It was Brundle's first Formula One drive of any description for a year and he did well to finish 9th, which was better than team-mate Riccardo Patrese who retired on lap 30.

After that one drive he returned to world sports car racing where he, and his Jaguar team, were in contention for the team and individual titles. They ended up winning both, giving Brundle his first world title.

Alex Caffi
Born: 18 March 1964, Italy
Lives: Bergamo, Italy
Formula One Teams: 1986–87 Osella; 1988 Dallara
Starts: 26
First Grand Prix: 1986 Italian GP
First Points: None yet
Wins: (0)
Best Finish: 7th   1988 Portuguese GP
Best World Championship Position: Never
   classified

Alex Caffi progressed to Formula One via Formula Three, but in three years, first with Osella and then Dallara, he has still to collect his first championship point.

He seems better suited to the Dallara and at Detroit (8th) and Estoril (7th) he was just outside the points.

Adrian Campos
Born: 17 June 1960, Valencia, Spain
Lives: Valencia, Spain
Formula One Teams: 1987–88 Minardi
Starts: 17
First Grand Prix: 1987 Brazilian GP
First Points: None yet
Wins: (0)
Best Finish: 14th   1987 Spanish GP
Best World Championship Position: Never
   classified

One of the two Spaniards in Formula One in 1988, Campos had no 'track record' before joining the big League. He had driven in Formula Three, but with little success and the same could be said about his flirtation with Formula 3000 in 1986. He joined the Minardi Grand Prix team in 1987 and his only finish was in his home Grand Prix at Jerez, when he finished last in 14th place. The 1988 season was no better and after failing to qualify for the Canadian Grand Prix, having done considerable damage to his car, he was sacked and replaced by the more experienced Pierluigi Martini. Campos immediately announced his retirement from Formula One.

Ivan Capelli
Born: 24 May 1963, Italy
Lives: Milan, Italy

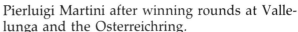

Formula One Teams: 1985 Tyrrell; 1986 AGS;
   1987–88 March
Starts: 34
First Grand Prix: 1985 European GP
First Points: 1985 Australian GP (4th)
Wins: (0)
Best Finish: 2nd   1988 Portuguese GP
Best World Championship Position: Jt. 7th   1988

In 1988 Italy's Ivan Capelli successfully made the transition from Formula Three, to Formula 3000 and then to Formula One.

The last European Formula Three champion in 1984, he followed that two years later by winning the Formula 3000 championship. By that time he had driven in the Tyrrell Formula One car when he took over from Stefan Bellof following the German's death. Capelli had only two drives with Tyrrell but in the second, the Australian Grand Prix, he collected his first championship points.

Although with the AGS Formula One team in 1986 Capelli spent a lot of the season racing in Formula 3000 with March, and won the championship from fellow Italians Emanuel Pirro and Pierluigi Martini after winning rounds at Vallelunga and the Osterreichring.

When March returned to Formula One in 1987 after a six year absence, they took Capelli with them and after a 'settling in' first year in 1988 the Judd-powered car put Capelli among the points and at Estoril they finished second to championship leader Alain Prost.

Eddie Cheever
Born: 10 January 1958, Phoenix, Arizona, USA
Lives: Rome/Monaco
Formula One Teams: 1978 Theodore/Hesketh;
   1979 not in Formula One; 1980 Osella; 1981
   Tyrrell; 1982 Ligier; 1983 Renault; 1984–85 Alfa
   Romeo; 1986 Lola; 1987–88 Arrows
Starts: 118
First Grand Prix: 1978 South African GP
   (Theodore)
First Points: 1981 United States GP (West) 5th
Wins: (0)
Best Finish: 2nd   1982 Detroit GP; 1983
   Canadian GP
Best World Championship Position: Jt. 6th   1983

Left: Adrian Campos in the Minardi during the 1987 Hungarian Grand Prix.

Right: The very experienced American Eddie Cheever. He has been on the Grand Prix scene since 1978 and is still waiting for his first win.

American Eddie Cheever seems to have been around a long time, yet he is only 30 years of age. He still enjoys his racing with the same boyish enthusiasm as he did when he came into Formula One in 1978 at the age of 20. However, despite his 'longevity', his first Grand Prix win still beckons, not that his career begins and ends at Formula One.

Runner-up to Rene Arnoux in the European Formula Two championship in 1977, Cheever has made his mark in the world of sports car racing and since partnering Riccardo Patrese to victory at Mugello in 1980, has won eight championship races. In 1988 he was involved in a great race for the championship with his Jaguar colleague Martin Brundle, before losing out to the Englishman.

With more than one hundred Grand Prix starts to his credit, there is no doubting Cheever's vast experience which goes back to the days when he was a karting champion, and a formidable Formula Three driver.

Always capable of getting among the points, his chance to make his mark among the elite of Formula One seems to have gone. He had his best season in 1983 when he finished second in the Canadian Grand Prix, which contributed six of his 22 championship points, his best haul in any one season. During the Canadian race he had transmission problems with the gears jumping out of fifth and finished the race with a badly blistered hand from holding it in gear.

Cheever can claim one record among the current Formula One drivers; he has had more teams than any other – nine!

Yannick Dalmas

Born: 28 July 1961, France
Lives: Le Beausset, nr. Toulon, France
Formula One Teams: 1987–88 Lola
Starts: 16
First Grand Prix: 1987 Mexican GP
First Points: None yet
Wins: (0)
Best Finish: 5th   1987 Australian GP
Best World Championship Position: Never classified

Yannick Dalmas had every good reason to enjoy the latter part of 1987. Having started the year driving in the Formula 3000 championship, he chalked up his first win at Pau in the March-Cosworth early in the season. On 11 October at Jarama he powered the March Formula 3000 car to victory for a second time. The following week Dalmas was in South America behind the wheel of the Lola Formula One car in Mexico. A month later at Adelaide, in the final race of the season,

he finished fifth but, because he had not competed in enough championship events, was not eligible for world championship points. Nevertheless, it heralded the end of a great season for the Frenchman.

Still with Lola in 1988 he had a bad year, largely due to his car being difficult to handle and he was forced to miss the final two races of 1988 when he caught Legionnaires Disease.

Andrea de Cesaris

Born: 31 May 1959, Rome, Italy
Lives: Rome
Formula One Teams: 1980 Alfa Romeo; 1981 McLaren; 1982–83 Alfa Romeo; 1984–85 Ligier; 1986 Minardi; 1987 Brabham; 1988 Rial
Starts: 119
First Grand Prix: 1980 Canadian GP
First Points: 1981 San Marino GP (6th)
Wins: (0)
Best Finish: 2nd   1983 German GP; South African GP
Best World Championship Position: 8th   1983

Andrea de Cesaris' big problem over the years has been keeping his car on the track. Now, however, he does not seem so prone to wrap it around the nearest piece of safety barrier!

Having finished runner-up in the 1979 British Formula Three championship, Alfa Romeo were the first Formula One team to give him a chance. After a year he went to McLaren before returning to the Italian manufacturers. Two years later he moved to Ligier but in 1985 they sacked him after he crashed their cars in testing, which included the multiple roll sequence seen every week at the start of BBC Television's *Grandstand* programme.

After that he struggled to find a team and Minardi were prepared to give him a chance in 1986. Since then he has been employed by Brabham and, in 1988, Rial. He is teaming up with Alex Caffi at Dallara in 1989 to give him his fifth team in as many years.

Despite his accident prone nature, de Cesaris has started more than 100 Grands Prix but still awaits his first win which looks as though it is now going to elude him.

Piercarlo Ghinzani

Born: 16 January 1952, Riviera d'Adda, Bergamo, Italy
Lives: Bergamo, Italy/Monaco
Formula One Teams: 1981–84 Osella; 1985 Toleman; 1986 Osella; 1987 Ligier; 1988 Zakspeed
Starts: 74
First Grand Prix: 1981 Belgian GP

Italy's Andrea de Cesaris.

Italian Piercarlo Ghinzani.

First Points: 1984 Dallas GP (5th)
Wins: (0)
Best Finish: 5th 1984 Dallas GP
Best World Championship Position: 19th 1984

A driver who excels at Formula Three or Formula Two is normally snapped up by a Formula One team, but Italy's Piercarlo Ghinzani was an exception. He won the European Formula Three title in 1977 and two years later captured the Italian Formula Two crown, but it was not until 1981 that he was given his first Formula One drive, for Osella in the Belgian Grand Prix.

After four seasons with the Italian manufacturer he moved to Toleman for a year before returning briefly to Osella. A year with Ligier in 1987 was followed by a season at Zakspeed.

Since registering a personal best of 5th in the 1984 Dallas Grand Prix, Ghinzani has failed to pick up a championship point. Despite his record, he is still a capable driver.

Mauricio Gugelmin
Born: 20 April 1963, Brazil
Lives: Egham, Surrey, England
Formula One Teams: 1988 March
Starts: 16
First Grand Prix: 1988 Brazilian GP

Another fine Brazilian talent, Maurico Gugelmin.

Left: Ah! That's where the nickname 'De Crasheris' comes from!

Right: Stefan Johansson having running repairs to his Ligier.

First Points: 1988 British GP (4th)
Wins: (0)
Best Finish: 4th 1988 British GP
Best World Championship Position: Jt. 12th 1988

First Brazil produced the great Emerson Fittipaldi, followed by Nelson Piquet and then Ayrton Senna. Is Mauricio Gugelmin the next to come off the production line? After only one season in Formula One it is hard to say, but judging by his performance in the 1988 British Grand Prix at Silverstone the answer could well be 'yes'.

Like Ayrton Senna two years before him, Gugelmin won the 1985 British Formula Three championship after successfully coming through Formula Ford following his arrival in Britain in 1982. Before making the transition to Formula One he had two years in Formula 3000 and won the opening round of the 1987 championship at Silverstone.

He joined the March Formula One team and had his first drive in his home Grand Prix, but it was not a happy return because his car refused to move off the start line. Three months later, however, it was a different story as his March left the grid and carried him to 4th place in the British Grand Prix and the first points for a delighted Gugelmin.

Stefan Johansson

Born: 8 September 1956, Vaxjo, Sweden
Lives: Monaco
Formula One Teams: 1983 Spirit; 1984 Tyrrell/Toleman; 1985–86 Ferrari; 1987 McLaren; 1988 Ligier
Starts: 70
First Grand Prix: 1983 British GP
First Points: 1984 Italian GP (4th)
Wins: (0)
Best Finish: 2nd 1985 Canadian GP; Detroit GP; 1987 Belgian GP; German GP
Best World Championship Position: 5th 1986

Stefan Johansson had a hard time trying to break into Formula One and when he did make it, he struggled to get hold of a competitive car to test his ability.

The 1980 British Formula Three champion, he followed that with moderate success at Formula Two. But the breakthrough to Grand Prix racing did not come until he was given a chance by the Spirit team in 1983 when he made his debut in the British Grand Prix at Silverstone.

The following season he drove for Tyrrell before the team was excluded from the championship; he then moved to Toleman. When Ferrari gave him a contract for the 1985 season it looked as though we would see the real Stefan

Johansson at last. But sadly, even the famous Italian car was not competitive enough. Nevertheless, the Swede finished second in back-to-back races at the Montreal and Detroit Grands Prix.

Still winless in 1986, Johansson managed to finish fifth in the world championship after getting among the points in seven rounds of the championship.

Although he did a good job for Ferrari, he was dropped by them at the end of 1986 in favour of Gerhard Berger. Johansson was then given a plum job with McLaren as second driver to the great Alain Prost. However, the pair had to watch the Williams duo of Piquet and Mansell dominate the championship. At the end of the season Johansson was replaced by the Brazilian Ayrton Senna.

The Swede joined his fifth team, Ligier, in 1988, and also competed in the world sports car championship, winning at Spa with Mauro Baldi; however the chance of Formula One glory appears to have passed by Stefan Johansson.

Nicola Larini
Born: 19 March 1964, Italy
Lives: Viareggio, Italy
Formula One Teams: 1987 Coloni; 1988 Osella
Starts: 11
First Grand Prix: 1987 Spanish GP
First Points: None yet
Wins: (0)
Best Finish: 9th 1988 Monaco GP
Best World Championship Position: Never classified

At 24, Nicola Larini was the second youngest driver on the Formula One circuit in 1988. The Italian Formula Three champion in 1986, Larini was given his first Formula One drive with Coloni at Monza the following year but failed to qualify. In his only other race, at Jerez, he started from the back of the grid and on lap 8 was the first of the 26 qualifiers to drop out of the race.

A move to Osella in 1988 saw an improvement and around the tight Monaco circuit he steered the car to 9th place; his best Grand Prix result.

Left: The experienced Swede Stefan Johansson.

Right: Down to a 2-handicap, Nigel Mansell is a first class golfer and in the 1988 Australian Open he made his debut in a senior golf tournament. He did well in the first round with a 77 but a damaged shoulder was too great a handicap after that. One of Nigel's best friends is Greg Norman.

Oscar Larrauri
Born: 19 August 1954, Argentina
Lives: Rosario, Argentina/Pavia, Italy
Formula One Teams: 1988 EuroBrun
Starts: 8
First Grand Prix: 1988 Brazilian GP
First Points: None yet
Wins: (0)
Best Finish: 13th   1988 Mexican GP
Best World Championship Position: Never
   classified

Oscar Larrauri won the 1982 European Formula Three championship. Surprisingly, it was another six years before he was to make his Formula One debut in the 1988 Brazilian Grand Prix at Rio de Janeiro. In between he helped Brun Motorsport to the Group C sports car world championship in 1986 with a win at Jerez.

His first Grand Prix team was Walter Brun's new EuroBrun team, and a first win, or indeed even a finish among the points, is still eagerly awaited to go alongside his Formula Three and sports car successes.

Nigel Mansell
Born: 8 August 1954, Upton-on-Severn,
   Worcestershire, England
Lives: Isle of Man
Formula One Teams: 1980–84 Lotus; 1985–88
   Williams
Starts: 118
First Grand Prix: 1980 Austrian GP
First Points: 1981 Belgian GP (3rd)
Wins (13):   1985 European GP; South African
   GP; 1986 Belgian GP; Canadian GP; French
   GP; British GP; Austrian GP; 1987 San Marino
   GP; French GP; British GP; Austrian GP,
   Spanish GP; Mexican GP
Best World Championship Position: 2nd   1986;
   1987

As James Hunt was midway through his successful world championship season in 1976, Nigel Mansell was setting out on his quest to emulate him and become the next British Champion.

Racing karts since 1968 Mansell, a former

Lucas Aerospace employee, had his first car race at Mallory Park in July 1976 when he won in a Formula Ford Hawke DL11. The following year his career nearly ended when he broke his neck in a Formula Ford accident. Within weeks he was back behind the wheel, despite being told he would probably never drive again because of his accident.

In 1978 he re-mortgaged his house in order to finance his venture into Formula Three. He first drove a Formula One car when he tested for Lotus at Paul Ricard in October 1979, and after a successful switch from Formula Three to Two in 1980 Mansell was given the chance of his first Grand Prix drive for Lotus in the 1980 Austrian Grand Prix. He had two more races that season before being offered the number two drive in Colin Chapman's team behind number one driver, Elio de Angelis.

When Mansell finished third in the Belgian Grand Prix British fans looked to him as their next world champion.

After the 1984 season Mansell left Lotus and teamed up with Frank Williams in a move that was to herald the start of a great period for both driver and team.

The inevitable first win came towards the end of the 1985 season when he won the European Grand Prix at Brands Hatch. Two weeks later he enjoyed back-to-back wins when he took the chequered flag at Kyalami. He finished sixth in the championship but both driver and car were ready for a serious assault on the world title the following year.

The Williams team looked forward to winning the Constructors' Championship before the final race of the season at Adelaide, but Mansell still needed to finish 4th or better to clinch the drivers' title. But who will ever forget the agony as his car blew a tyre on lap 64? Mansell did a magnificent job to avert a major disaster, but he went out of the race with his championship dream in tatters. He could only sit and watch as Alain Prost went on to win his second successive title.

Mansell was determined to capture the crown in 1987 but a shunt while practising for the Japanese Grand Prix aggravated his back and he was forced to miss the Japanese race and the final one of the season at Adelaide, which meant he waved goodbye to yet another championship after being in contention for so long.

Sadly, with the loss of the Honda power behind the Williams team, Mansell's car was not competitive enough in 1988 although Mansell showed signs of personal brilliance, particularly in the thrilling British Grand Prix at Silverstone. For 1989 Nigel has moved to Ferrari and with it rests his next chance to win the world title, and thus fulfil his single-minded ambition to become Britain's first world champion since James Hunt.

Mansell left a good job and took the gamble of re-mortgaging his house to finance his thirst for success, and as his temperament is centred around a determined will, he is now reaping the rewards of those decisions as he stands among the elite of motor racing.

Left: The best British driver in recent years, Nigel Mansell.

Right: Nigel Mansell in his familiar Williams but sadly, after four successful years, the partnership ended in 1988 when Nigel went to Ferrari.

Pierluigi Martini
Born: 23 April 1961, Bologna, Italy
Lives: Ravenna, Italy
Formula One Teams: 1985 Minardi; 1986–87 Not
  in Formula One; 1988 Minardi
Starts: 24
First Grand Prix: 1985 Brazilian GP
First Points: 1988 Detroit GP (6th)
Wins: (0)
Best Finish: 6th   1988 Detroit GP
Best World Championship Position: Jt. 16th   1988

Italian Pierluigi Martini was recalled to Formula One action in 1988 when he replaced Spaniard Adrian Campos in the Minardi team. He was given his first Formula One chance with the team in 1985 but has not been a regular Grand Prix driver, and his sole world championship point was in the 1988 Detroit Grand Prix.

The 1983 European Formula Three champion, Martini concentrated on Formula 3000 in 1986 and 1987 and finished third in the championship in the first of those years, following wins at Imola and Mugello. While awaiting his recall to Formula One he continued to drive in Formula 3000 and was also the Minardi test driver.

Stefano Modena
Born: 12 May 1953, Modena, Italy
Lives: Modena
Formula One Teams: 1987 Brabham; 1988
  EuroBrun
Starts: 11
First Grand Prix: 1987 Australian GP
First Points: None yet
Wins: (0)
Best Finish: 11th   1988 Hungarian GP
Best World Championship Position: Never
  classified

A former world junior kart champion, Stefano Modena was given his first Grand Prix drive in a Brabham at Adelaide in 1987. Ironically, it was the last race before their withdrawal from Formula One. Outstanding in Formula 3000, Modena won the 1987 European title helped by two wins at Vallelunga and Birmingham.

Following Brabham's withdrawal he teamed up with the EuroBrun team but struggled to get the car on to the starting grid in most races. Certainly very talented, given the right machinery, Modena could well be a star of the future.

Satoru Nakajima
Born: 23 February 1953, Okajaki, Japan
Lives: Walton-on-Thames, England
Formula One Teams: 1987–88 Lotus
Starts: 30
First Grand Prix: 1987 Brazilian GP

Lotus's Japanese-born driver Satoru Nakajima.

First Points: 1987 San Marino GP (6th)
Wins: (0)
Best Finish: 4th   1987 British GP
Best World Championship Position: Jt. 11th
  1987

When Satoru Nakajima finished 6th in the 1987 San Marino Grand Prix (his second Grand Prix) he became the first Japanese driver to collect points in the world championship.

His entry into Formula One in 1987 was via the usual channels, Formula Three, Formula Two, and Formula 3000, but he enjoyed little success before taking the big step into the top formula. He was given the chance to drive with the Lotus Formula One team as part of the package that gave them Honda engines.

After his initial success at San Marino he got among the points again on three more occasions, including a personal best 4th at Silverstone, and 6th in his home Grand Prix in Japan.

Having been number two driver to Ayrton Senna in 1987 Nakajima was second string to Nelson Piquet at Lotus the following year. Piquet finished 3rd in the opening championship race at Rio de Janeiro, and Nakajima came 6th.

Another of the many Italians in Formula One, Alessandro Nannini who will be enjoying his second term at Benetton in 1989.

This gave the team and Nakajima some hope but that was to be the Japanese driver's only point of the season, and one of only a handful collected by the Brazilian.

Alessandro Nannini
Born: 7 July 1959, Italy
Lives: Siena, Italy
Formula One Teams: 1986–87 Minardi; 1988 Benetton
Starts: 47
First Grand Prix: 1986 Brazilian GP
First Points: 1988 San Marino GP (6th)
Wins: (0)
Best Finish: 3rd   1988 British GP, Spanish GP
Best World Championship Position: Jt. 9th   1988

Yet another Italian in Formula One, Alessandro Nannini knew that with the right car he could prove his worth. And he did just that in 1988.

An ex-Formula Two and sports car driver, Nannini had his first Grand Prix drive at Rio in 1986. After spending two years with the not-so-reliable Minardi team he switched to the fast-emerging Benetton team and in the San Marino Grand Prix, the second of the 1988 season, he

got among the points for the first time in his career, finishing 6th.

At Silverstone a couple of months later he finished 3rd, a result he repeated in Spain later in the season as he proved himself a capable member of the team behind leader Thierry Boutsen.

He has always had the talent to succeed in Formula One and with Benetton becoming more competitive all the time, Nannini can look forward to his first Grand Prix success in 1989.

Jonathan Palmer
Born: 7 November 1956, London, England
Lives: Dogmersfield, nr. Fleet, Hampshire, England
Formula One Teams: 1983 Williams; 1984 RAM; 1985–86 Zakspeed; 1987–88 Tyrrell
Starts: 68
First Grand Prix: 1983 European GP
First Points: 1987 Monaco GP (5th)
Wins: (0)
Best Finish: 4th   1987 Australian GP
Best World Championship Position: Jt. 11th 1987

With nearly seventy Grands Prix to his credit, Jonathan Palmer has had more Formula One experience than many people realize.

Educated at Brighton College, Palmer won a special engineering award for his design of a 70mph (112.6kph) Kart. Eventually he turned to medicine and became a qualified doctor only to leave the profession in 1981 to concentrate on racing full-time. His decision paid instant dividends because he won the British Formula Three title that year.

Two years later Palmer won the European Formula Two title and that same year made his Grand Prix debut in a Williams at Brands Hatch in the European Grand Prix. However, getting a regular drive in Formula One the following season was not as easy as it should have been for a driver of Palmer's immense talent. John MacDonald wanted him at RAM, but the team needed money. If Palmer could bring sponsorship with him he could have a regular drive. With the same determination as he shows behind the wheel, Palmer went out and sold himself and came back with enough money to make him a RAM Formula One driver.

After only one season with RAM he moved to Zakspeed for two years before swapping teams with Martin Brundle and joining Ken Tyrrell in 1987. In the meantime, Palmer dovetailed his Formula One activities with sports car drives and with Jan Lammers at Brands Hatch in 1984 he took their Porsche to victory. The following

The great backdrop at the 1988 Brazilian Grand Prix for Alessandro Nannini and his Benetton.

year Palmer was runner-up in the Le Mans 24 Hour race.

In Formula One he won the Jim Clark Cup for drivers of non-turbo cars in 1987, and helped the Tyrrell team to the inaugural Colin Chapman Cup, again for non-turbo cars. Those championships were not contested again in 1988 and, apart from getting among the points a few times, Palmer had little to show from the next season.

With the end of the turbo revolution and provided Ken Tyrrell can come up with a competitive car, the 'flying doctor' could well challenge Nigel Mansell as top Briton in 1989.

Riccardo Patrese
Born: 17 April 1954, Padua, Italy
Lives: Padua/Monaco
Formula One Teams: 1977 Shadow; 1978–81 Arrows; 1982–83 Brabham; 1984–85 Alfa

Nigel Mansell's partner at Williams in 1988, Riccardo Patrese became the team's number one driver in 1989.

Romeo; 1986 Brabham; 1987 Brabham/ Williams; 1988 Williams
Starts: 176
First Grand Prix: 1977 Monaco GP
First Points: 1977 Japanese GP (6th)
Wins (2): 1982 Monaco GP; 1983 South African GP
Best World Championship Position: 9th 1980; 1983

The most experienced man in Formula One, Riccardo Patrese has more than 170 drives to his credit and started the 1989 season as the most experienced driver of all-time, surpassing the 176 total of Jacques Laffite and Graham Hill in his first start of the new season.

The 1974 world karting champion and 1976 European Formula Three champion, Patrese has been in Formula One since having his first drive with the Shadow team at Monaco in 1977 – four days after his son Simone was born.

Despite his long career, however, he has had only two wins, at Monaco in 1982 and at Kyalami the following year. He has never finished better than 9th in the world championship.

Dour and unsmiling he has a history of controversial incidents on the track, stemming largely from his impetuous nature and unpredictability when it comes to overtaking. One such incident at Monza in 1978 resulted in a long drawn-out legal battle which saw Patrese charged with the manslaughter of Ronnie Peterson in the first such trial of its kind in motor racing history.

At the start of the Italian Grand Prix, Patrese, trying to find room on a narrow part of the circuit, caught James Hunt's McLaren, which in turn clipped Peterson's Lotus which caused the Swede's fatal accident. Patrese and a Monza track official, Gianni Restelli, were both charged with Peterson's manslaughter. In October 1981 they were acquitted.

Patrese always wanted to drive for Ferrari but that dream never materialized. After five seasons with Shadow and then Arrows he spent two years with Brabham, during which time he had his two wins. He moved to Alfa Romeo in 1984 but in 1986 returned to Brabham after the Italian team quit Formula One.

He was released from Brabham at the end of 1987 and became Nigel Mansell's new partner at Williams. After Mansell moved to Ferrari in 1989 Patrese was retained and was joined by Thierry Boutsen.

In the early 1980s Patrese enjoyed success at endurance racing and won seven world sports car championship races between 1980–85. Three of his successes were with Michele Alboreto.

Nelson Piquet
Born: 17 August 1952, Rio de Janeiro, Brazil
Lives: Monaco
Formula One Teams: 1978 Ensign/McLaren; 1979–
    85 Brabham; 1986–87 Williams; 1988 Lotus
Starts: 157
First Grand Prix: 1978 German GP
First Points: 1979 Dutch GP (4th)
Wins: (20)   1980 United States (West) GP;
    Dutch GP; Italian GP; 1981 Argentine GP; San
    Marino GP; German GP; 1982 Canadian GP;
    1983 Brazilian GP; Italian GP; European GP;
    1984 Canadian GP; Detroit GP; 1985 French
    GP; 1986 Brazilian GP; Hungarian GP;
    German GP; Italian GP; 1987 German GP;
    Hungarian GP; Italian GP
Best World Championship Position: Champion
    1981; 1983; 1987

With three world titles to his credit, Brazil's
Nelson Piquet can rightly claim to be one of the
all-time great drivers, particularly in such a competitive age of motor racing.

Although his number of world titles falls short
of the record five of Argentina's Juan Manuel
Fangio, he still shares three wins with such
greats as Jack Brabham, Jackie Stewart and Niki
Lauda.

Piquet possesses enormous natural talent but is
a complex person by nature and isolates himself
from the furore that goes with Formula One
Grand Prix racing. He gave up a potentially good
lawn tennis career to take up kart racing in 1970
and it was then that he changed his name from
Nelson Souto Maior to Piquet (his mother's
maiden name) so that his father wouldn't find
out about his kart racing involvement. Dr. Estacio
de Souto Maior was the former Brazilian national
tennis coach and understandably he expected
his son to make a career in tennis. But Piquet's
decision to abandon tennis proved right because
in 1972 he was the Brazilian Kart Champion
before later becoming Brazilian Super Vee
Champion in 1976.

Third in the 1977 European Formula Three
championship, Piquet won the BP British title
the following year. That same year he competed
in the German Grand Prix in an Ensign. He had
three more drives that season with McLaren before starting a seven-year partnership with the
Brabham Formula One team, during which time
he won two world titles, and enjoyed 13 Grand
Prix wins.

He first came close to winning the world title
in 1980 in the new Brabham BT49 but finished
second to Alan Jones. By then Piquet was
Brabham team-leader following the retirement
of Niki Lauda.

Piquet's three world titles have all been close
affairs: in 1981 he snatched the title by one point
from Carlos Reutemann by finishing 5th in the
Las Vegas Grand Prix. Two years later his four
points for finishing 3rd in the South African
Grand Prix were enough for him to overhaul
Alain Prost in the last race of the season and win
the title by two points. And in 1987 he took the
title from team-mate Nigel Mansell after the
Briton missed the last two races of the season
following an accident while practising for the
Japanese Grand Prix.

Despite two successful years at Williams in
1986 and 1987, when he won his third world
title, his tenancy in the Williams car was marred
by unpleasantness between himself and Mansell
as both men were determined to be the team's
number one driver. That friction did nothing to
help team morale and in 1988 Piquet moved to
Lotus.

Nelson Piquet of Brazil, world champion in 1981,
1983 and 1987.

As well as winning 20 Grands Prix, Piquet has one sports car world championship success to his credit when, with co-driver Hans Stuck, he won at the Nurburgring in 1981.

Alain Prost

Born: 24 February 1955, St. Chamond, nr. St. Etienne, France
Lives: Yens, Switzerland
Formula One Teams: 1980 McLaren; 1981–83 Renault; 1984–88 McLaren
Starts: 137
First Grand Prix: 1980 Argentine GP
First Points: 1980 Argentine GP (6th)
Wins: (35)   1981 French GP; Dutch GP; Italian GP; 1982 South African GP; Brazilian GP; 1983 French GP; Belgian GP; British GP; Austrian GP; 1984 Brazilian GP; San Marino GP; Monaco GP; German GP; Dutch GP; European GP; Portuguese GP; 1985 Brazilian GP; Monaco GP; British GP; Austrian GP; Italian GP; 1986 San Marino GP; Monaco GP; Austrian GP; Australian GP; 1987 Brazilian GP; Belgian GP; Portuguese GP; 1988 Brazilian GP; Monaco GP; Mexican GP; French GP; Portuguese GP; Spanish GP; Australian GP
Best World Championship Position: Champion 1985; 1986

The most successful Grand Prix driver of all time, Alain Prost surpassed Jackie Stewart's record of 27 wins in 1987 and is still adding to that total which has now gone past the 30-mark.

One of the sport's nice guys, Prost is known as 'The Professor' because of his calculated approach to his driving. He won the first of his world titles in 1985 when he became the first Frenchman to capture the coveted crown. The following year he became the first man since Jack Brabham in 1959–60 to win successive titles.

He had threatened to lift the world title since winning his first Grand Prix in 1981. He was runner-up by two points to Nelson Piquet in the 1983 championship and the following year was pipped by his McLaren team-mate Niki Lauda by a mere half-a-point. But those two disappointments turned to joy in 1985 when he won his first title.

Alain Prost could have enjoyed a successful career in professional football but chose motor racing instead. He first attracted attention in 1976 when he won the French Formula Renault title winning 12 of the 13 rounds. The following year he won the European title before switching to Formula Three.

In 1979 he won the European Formula Three title and the following year he started alongside

Above left: Brazil's second world champion after Emerson Fittipaldi, Nelson Piquet.

Left: Nelson Piquet in the Williams FW11 at the 1987 British Grand Prix at Silverstone where he finished second to team-mate Nigel Mansell.

Right: The likeable Frenchman, Alain Prost, twice world champion and three times runner-up.

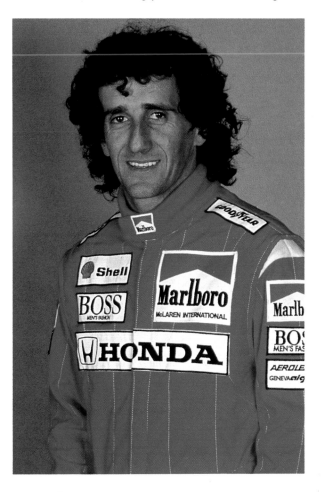

Above: Alain Prost in the 1988 McLaren MP4/4, the most successful car in the history of Formula One.

Left: Alain Prost holding aloft the magnificent trophy for winning the 1988 Brazilian Grand Prix.

Next page: A great view over Alain Prost's shoulder during the 1988 British Grand Prix at Silverstone.

John Watson in the McLaren Formula One team, and picked up a point at Buenos Aires on his Grand Prix debut.

The next season he replaced Jean-Pierre Jabouille at Renault, and how appropriate it was that Prost should win his first Grand Prix at Dijon-Prenois, home of the French Grand Prix. That was the start of a run that has seen the likeable Frenchman win every season, and since then he has won once in every four races, a remarkable average.

After three years with Renault Prost returned to Marlboro-McLaren in 1984 and has been with them ever since, winning all but nine of his Grands Prix in one of their cars.

Alain Prost is the ultimate professional and a credit to the sport. In 1988 he had the promising young talent of Ayrton Senna alongside him in the McLaren team and the rivalry between the two drivers was keen and intense. Sadly for Prost, for the third time he lost the title in the final race of the season as the Brazilian just beat him to the title.

Luis Perez Sala

Born: 15 May 1959, Barcelona, Spain
Lives: Barcelona, Spain
Formula One Teams: 1988 Minardi
Starts: 14
First Grand Prix: 1988 Brazilian GP
First Points: None yet
Wins: (0)
Best Finish: 8th   1988 Portuguese GP
Best World Championship Position: Never
   classified

With an outstanding Formula 3000 career behind him, Luis Sala was expected to make a bigger impression on Formula One than he has.

He won two rounds of the 1986 Formula 3000 championship, including the inaugural Birmingham Super Prix. And in 1987 he won two more races, at Donington and Le Mans, before finishing runner-up in the championship to Stefano Modena.

However, his Formula One baptism was with the less than competitive Minardi team in the Brazilian Grand Prix and he has still to finish higher than 8th.

Jean-Louis Schlesser

Born: France
Lives: France
Formula One Teams: 1988 Williams
Starts: 1
First Grand Prix: 1988 Italian GP
First Points: None yet
Wins: (0)

Best Finish: 11th   1988 Italian GP
Best World Championship Position: Never
   classified

Jean-Louis Schlesser has had only one world championship drive, but he did enough in front of the enthusiastic fans at Monza to become the next in a long line of favourites adopted by Italian followers. He got the drive in Nigel Mansell's Williams because first 'reserve' Martin Brundle was away on sports car duties with Jaguar.

Schlesser, a nephew of the late Jo Schlesser, has been around for some time but this was only his second Formula One drive; the first being in the non-championship Race of Champions in 1983 driving a RAM-March. Since then he has test driven for Williams and proved to be a popular member of the team. But, like Brundle, he has been concentrating on the World Sports Car Championship and in 1988 he challenged Brundle for the title only to lose to the Briton.

At Monza Schlesser started from 22nd position on the grid but drove steadily to finish in 11th place, despite a spin on lap 50 which involved race leader Ayrton Senna who was forced to retire.

Bernd Schneider

Born: 20 July 1964, West Germany
Lives: Saarbrucken, West Germany
Formula One Teams: 1988 Zakspeed
Starts: 6
First Grand Prix: 1988 Mexican GP
First Points: None yet
Wins: (0)
Best Finish: 12th   1988 German GP
Best World Championship Position: Never
   classified

The baby of the 1988 Formula One drivers, Germany's Bernd Schneider was two months short of his 24th birthday when he made his Grand Prix debut at Mexico City.

A former world junior karting champion he took up single seater racing in 1984 and was the German Formula Three champion in 1987. He was on the verge of progressing to Formula 3000 when Zakspeed offered him a drive in one of their Formula One cars in 1988. The transition has been a difficult one and a year in Formula 3000 would have done him no harm.

Ayrton Senna

Born: 21 March 1960, Sao Paulo, Brazil
Lives: Monaco
Formula One Teams: 1984 Toleman; 1985–87
   Lotus; 1988 McLaren
Starts: 78

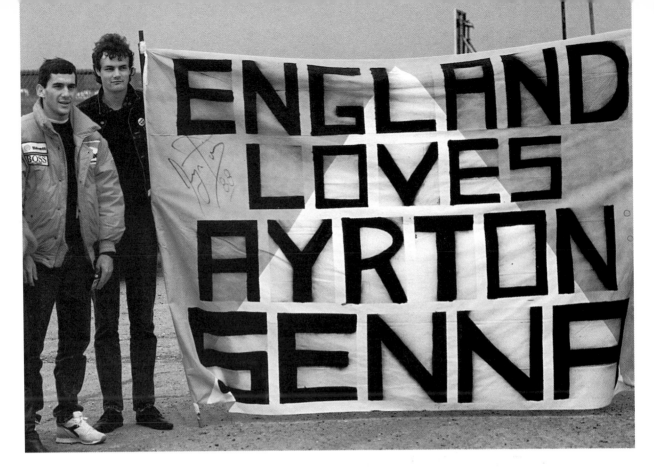

Above: What more can one add to the banner . . .?

Left: Winning a Grand Prix appears to be a lot easier than getting into a hammock for Ayrton Senna!

Right: Be careful Ayrton, it may be Ming! Ayrton Senna after winning the 1988 Hungarian Grand Prix.

Next page: The 1988 world champion Ayrton Senna in his equally successful McLaren MP4/4.

First Grand Prix: 1984 Brazilian GP
First Points: 1984 South African GP (6th)
Wins: (14)   1985 Portuguese GP; Belgian GP;
   1986 Spanish GP; Detroit GP; 1987 Monaco
   GP; United States GP; 1988 San Marino GP;
   Canadian GP; United States GP; British GP;
   German GP; Hungarian GP; Belgian GP;
   Japanese GP
Best World Championship Position: Champion
   1988

Following Fittipaldi and Piquet, the next great Brazilian driver is Ayrton Senna da Silva. He dropped the da Silva part of his name, but whatever he chooses to call himself, there is no denying his amazing natural talent.

A former runner-up in the kart world championship, he was a champion at Formula Ford in both Britain and Europe. But it was in 1983 that he really took the motor racing world by storm when he powered his way to the British Formula Three title. On his way to winning the championship he won a record 12 rounds, including a staggering 9 in succession.

It is hardly surprising that he became the hottest property in Formula One, but with a limited number of drives available, he started his 'new' career with the lesser known Toleman team and had his first drive in his home Grand Prix.

The Toleman may have been no match for the likes of McLaren, Ferrari, Lotus, Brabham and Renault, but with the great skill of Senna behind the wheel he pushed it to 2nd place in the rain-interrupted Monaco Grand Prix and to 3rd place at Brands Hatch and Estoril.

A move to Lotus in 1985 brought the anticipated first win, at Estoril. That was the first of 14 wins for the talented Brazilian. Despite three successful years at Lotus in which Senna won six races and challenged for the world title, his first real chance of a title came when he teamed up with Alain Prost at McLaren in 1988.

These two were so dominant that it was a foregone conclusion that they would win the Constructors' Championship long before the season was over but the battle for the drivers' crown would be decided in the final race, and it was between the two team-mates.

Senna had an outstanding season: he surpassed the record of Jim Clark and Prost by winning eight races, and his 13 pole positions was also a new record.

The 1988 season ended on a high note for Senna as he beat his team-mate to the title and became the third Brazilian to lift the world crown. Like his other fellow countrymen, they have not been content in winning one title, they have wanted more. Senna is no different.

Ayrton Senna has an insatiable appetite for success and in his early days of Formula One needed to be held by the reins because of his impatience to succeed. Now, he demands the best treatment from his team and in return he gives them his all.

Philippe Streiff

Born: 26 June 1955, Grenoble, France
Lives: Lausanne, Switzerland
Formula One Teams: 1984 Renault; 1985 Ligier;
   1986–87 Tyrrell; 1988 AGS
Starts: 53
First Grand Prix: 1984 Portuguese GP
First Points: 1985 Australian GP (3rd)
Wins: (0)
Best Finish: 3rd   1985 Australian GP
Best World Championship Position: Jt. 13th   1986

The likeable Philippe Streiff turned full circle when he teamed up with AGS in 1988. He had previously driven for them in his Formula Two days in the early 1980s, and his return renewed a partnership with Henri Julien.

A former French Formula Three champion, Streiff made the natural progression to Formula Two before having his first drive in Formula One, with Renault at Estoril in the final race of the 1984 season. Earlier in the year Streiff finished third in the Le Mans 24 Hour race with Hobbs and Van Der Merwe.

Ligier gave him four drives in their Grand Prix car in 1985 and he picked up his first points for finishing 3rd at Adelaide, his best finish to date.

He spent two seasons with Tyrrell before joining AGS in 1988. Streiff is a competent driver and perhaps we shall see his true ability emerge in 1989 when the sport becomes more a test of the driver's skill with the abolition of the turbocharged car.

Aguri Suzuki

Born: 1960, Tokyo, Japan
Formula One Teams: 1988 Lola
First Grand Prix: 1988 Japanese GP
First Points: None yet
Wins: (0)
Best finish: 16th   1988 Japanese GP
Best World Championship Position: Never classified

A stand-in for the ill Yannick Dalmas in the Lola team, Aguri Suzuki gave the home Japanese fans plenty to cheer about at his Grand Prix debut in 1988. He started from the 10th row of the grid alongside team-mate Philippe Alliot.

Despite spinning the car three times during the race he finished a commendable 16th, three laps down on the winner Ayrton Senna.

He is expected to get a regular drive in the Zakspeed team in 1989 alongside Bernd Schneider.

Gabriele Tarquini

Born: 2 March 1962, Italy
Lives: Guilianova, Italy
Formula One Teams: 1987 Osella; 1988 Coloni
Starts: 9
First Grand Prix: 1987 San Marino GP
First Points: None
Wins: (0)
Best Finish: 8th   1988 Canadian GP
Best World Championship Position: Never classified

Another of the many Italians in Formula One in 1988, Tarquini is a former world karting cham-

pion who had a spell in Formula 3000 without any reasonable success – hardly the right pedigree for a Formula One driver.

Tarquini had one drive for Osella in 1987 at Imola and in 1988 he drove for the Coloni team but had problems in pre-qualifying for most races. His best finish was in the Canadian Grand Prix when he finished 8th.

Derek Warwick

Born: 27 August 1954, Alresford, nr. Colchester, England
Lives: Jersey
Formula One Teams: 1981–83 Toleman; 1984–85 Renault; 1986 Brabham; 1987–88 Arrows
Starts: 100
First Grand Prix: 1981 Las Vegas GP
First Points: 1983 Dutch GP (4th)
Wins: (0)
Best Finish: 2nd 1984 Belgian GP; 1984 British GP
Best World Championship Position: Jt. 7th 1988

A former stock car champion before going into Formula Three and Two, Warwick's baptism in Formula One was a struggle with the new Toleman team in 1981, but he has since shown himself to be a reliable member of the Formula One 'circus'.

The 1978 Vandervell British Formula Three champion, Warwick was runner-up in the European Formula Two championship two years later before getting into Formula One.

He spent three years with Toleman before joining Renault in 1984. The move was expected to show an upturn in Warwick's fortunes but sadly the French manufacturer was on the downward slide at the time and, despite finishing 2nd at Zolder and Brands Hatch three months later, Warwick never got the win he deserved. That win is still pending despite a move to Brabham in 1986 when he joined the team as a replacement for Elio de Angelis who lost his life testing; Warwick would have been without a drive had Brabham not called upon his services.

The final race of the 1988 season was Warwick's 100th of his career and he is only the fourth man to have one hundred drives without a win: one of the other three is his 1989 teammate Eddie Cheever! Now, if ever there was an incentive for both drivers in the new season that is it . . .

'The Hustler' Gabriele Tarquini (left) with fellow drivers (l to r) Stefan Johansson, Bruno Giacomelli and Andrea de Cesaris.

Right: Britain's Derek Warwick. He is staying with Arrows in 1989 and will be hoping to get his first win after eight seasons in Formula One.

6. The Grand Prix Circuits

Since the formula one world championship was instituted in 1950 a total of 53 different circuits have staged races in 22 countries across five continents.

The severity of a circuit is, naturally, the test of a driver's skill. But these days, it is equally a test of the car's ability. The twisting Estoril circuit in Portugal is testament to that. In the Portuguese Grand Prix in 1988, for example, the non-turbo powered cars came to the fore and chased the turbo-charged McLaren of Alain Prost all the way to the finish line. The reason: the presence of many twisting bends and curves, and the lack of long straights which have proved to be advantageous to the turbo powered cars.

Over the years circuits have been a variety of shapes and sizes. Early races took place on open roads and were often straight races from one European city to another. One needs little imagination to see what sort of dangers there would be if the 200mph (321kph) McLarens raced from, say, Paris to Madrid today! As a result of the obvious dangers, road racing was banned in many countries and consequently it was necessary to construct purpose-built circuits.

The first of the great purpose-built circuits was **Brooklands**. Built on Lord Northcliffe's estate near Weybridge, Surrey, it opened in 1907 and was the home of British motor sport for thirty years. It was the scene of many record-breaking attempts, and was also used as a testing ground for leading manufacturers who pushed their road cars to the limit. Being the first purpose-built circuit the designer had little knowledge of motor racing circuits and consequently his design was based on a horse race track. The circuit was, therefore, more or less oval.

The main features of Brooklands however, were the two steep banked bends known as the Byfleet Banking and the Members Banking which peaked to a height of 29ft (9m). Such severe banking would never be allowed in today's safety conscious world of motor racing, but in the 1930s it provided a great spectacle as the magnificent Bugattis sped around the track.

The track surface was made of a flimsy 6in (15.24cm) layer of concrete and was 100ft (30.48m) wide. Understandably, because of its constant wear and tear during the racing season, extensive repairs were carried out each winter. The full circuit measured 2.77 miles (4.45km), and within the main outer course were two other shorter circuits.

Brooklands staged the first British Grand Prix in 1926 but sadly, by the time world championship racing arrived, the circuit was closed after being requisitioned by the Vickers Aircraft company during the war, and later bought by them in 1946.

In the years leading up to the last war Brook-

Previous page: The spectacular setting of the Rio de Janeiro circuit.

Right: The famous Nurburgring in the 1920s. The tree-lined trackside was one of its major features.

Next page: Grand Prix racing came to Las Vegas in 1981 when the car park of Caesar's Palace was turned into a racing circuit.

lands had to share the British Grand Prix with **Donington Park**, set in the grounds of the 17th century Donington Hall in Leicestershire. Opened in 1931 it was originally 2.19 miles (3.5km) long but was extended the following year to 2.55 miles (4.1km) and in 1937 to 3.125 miles (5km).

Set in English parkland it was the first of the present-day road circuits built on private land. Its variety of bends, steep undulating sections, and short straights made it a real road circuit. It staged the British Grand Prix between 1935–38. The 1937 race saw the appearance of the first great German cars in Britain as the Auto Unions and Mercedes-Benz dominated the race.

Like Brooklands, the circuit was requisitioned during the war, and was under the control of the army for some time after the hostilities. It looked as though racing was never to return to the famous circuit, despite several attempts to have the track restored. But in 1974 local rose magnate Tom Wheatcroft bought the circuit and in July 1978 a crowd of 30,000 turned up to watch the first international meeting at the new circuit. It has not been used for a Formula One world championship race, but most other forms of racing, both cars and bikes, still take place at Donington and there is a magnificent motor museum there.

Other famous circuits in the pre-world championship days included the French tracks at Pau

and Montlhery. **Montlhery**, situated near Paris, was opened in 1924. It was modelled on Brooklands although its lap at 1.606 miles (2.5km) was considerably shorter. However, its steep banking, even more severe than at Brooklands, was a major feature, and the short straights made it a testing circuit.

Built on a private estate, the circuit could be extended if necessary by utlizing the roads within the grounds of the estate, and could stretch to a 7.767 mile (12.4km) lap. Because it could be extended, the circuit was used for the French Grand Prix eight times between 1925–37. The road surface was a lot smoother than Brooklands and consequently many speed records were set at Montlhery.

After the war the autodrome remained in existence for use by the French car industry and the army for vehicle testing before its eventual closure in the 1970s.

Another famous French circuit was centred around the southern French town of **Pau**. Two circuits have borne the name of the town over the years; one a round-the-houses circuit, the other a triangular shaped road circuit.

The 9.86 mile (15.875km) road circuit was used for the French Grand Prix on just one occasion, in 1930. The round-the-houses circuit was established three years later and was used for the Pau Grand Prix 1933–49.

Pau staged its last Formula One race in 1963, which was won by Jim Clark. The town still stages events, notably Formula Three and Formula 3000.

Since the start of the world championship in 1950 there has been a huge variety of circuits, including one laid out on the car park of Caesar's Palace, Las Vegas. It may have been an unimaginative circuit, but it still brought the thrill of Grand Prix racing to the famous American gambling centre. Following is a look at all the circuits that have been used since the start of the world championship in 1950 and how they compare in shape, size and difficulty.

Germany

The most famous of all German circuits is the **Nurburgring**. Now a shadow of its former self the circuit measured a mammoth 14.189 miles (22.83km) at one time, making it the second longest ever to be used for a world championship race (for longest see *Italy* on page 165).

A road circuit set in the Eifel district of Germany near Koblenz, the Nurburgring, with seventy-plus twists and turns, was one of the most demanding and exhausting circuits for a

Other features of the Nurburgring were the steeped, banked bends.

driver because it demanded 100 per cent concentration for long spells. To add to its already natural hazards an artificial bank was included at one stage.

Built in the 1920s to give work to some of the unemployed, the first German Grand Prix was held at Nurburgring in 1927 and was won by Otto Merz in a Mercedes. Every German Grand Prix up to the outbreak of the war was staged at 'The Ring'. When the world championship started Germany was not included in the calendar. It was given a Grand Prix the following year and, of course, the Nurburgring was chosen as the venue.

A dangerous circuit, the Nurburgring is believed to have claimed the lives of more than fifty drivers over the years including Formula One drivers Onofre Marimon (Argentina), Peter Collins (Great Britain), Carol Godin de Beaufort (Holland) and John Taylor (Great Britain). After Taylor's death in 1966 some new bends were added in an attempt to make the circuit slower, notably the addition of the Bremscurve near the start at Tiergarten.

Drivers constantly complained about the famous circuit despite its long history, and in 1970 it was removed from the Grand Prix calendar for a year while the trees, rocks and fences which lined the road were removed to improve visibility. Their removal certainly made the circuit safer when it returned to the racing calendar in 1971.

However, while most Grand Prix circuits measured approximately 3–3½ miles (4.8–5.6km) the Nurburgring was still a monster at 14.167 miles (22.795km).

One of its biggest critics was Austrian Niki Lauda and in 1976 he nearly lost his life at 'The Ring'. That was the last Grand Prix over the 'old' circuit and moves were made to redesign the Nurburgring. The new, shorter, circuit at 2.8 miles (4.51km) reopened on 12 May 1984 when it hosted a twelve-hour festival to mark its return after a £20 million facelift. Famous names from the past like Stirling Moss, Jack Brabham, Phil Hill and John Surtees competed in this nostalgic event. The new circuit hosted the European Grand Prix five months later and in 1985 hosted the German Grand Prix again. But that was to be its last world championship race. The once dreaded but thrilling Nurburgring was no longer a testing and demanding course and drivers had only to memorize six left-hand and eight right-hand bends to complete the new circuit.

The current home of the German Grand Prix is **Hockenheim**, near Mannheim, a small town in the south of Germany.

Built in 1939 Hockenheim closed during the war and reopened in 1947 when it staged Formula Two and Three racing. It closed again in 1955 and was completely rebuilt in 1966 following the routing of an autobahn through the original complex.

Sadly Hockenheim is remembered as the

course that killed Jim Clark, during a Formula Two race in 1968. Following his death the tree-lined circuit had safety barriers added and in 1970, after the Nurburgring's failure to comply with the Grand Prix Drivers' Association's safety requests, Hockenheim was used for the first of its twelve Grands Prix. It was felt to be safer than the Nurburgring, and the long, fast, right-hand Ostkurve at the far end of the track offered the only serious challenge to the drivers.

Compared with many circuits the Hockenheimring is relatively boring. Its two long straights are broken by chicanes and the most interesting part of the circuit is the sharp left-handed Sachskurve, followed by the two right-handers leading into the finishing straight. It is a test of a car's staying power rather than a driver's ability.

The Nurburgring returned as host to the German Grand Prix in 1971 but was replaced by Hockenheim once more in 1977, since when Hockenheim has been the regular home of the race, with the exception of 1985 when the new 'Ring' was used.

The 1966 circuit measured 4.218 miles (6.787km); the current circuit is slightly longer at 4.224 miles (6.796km).

Hockenheim and Nurburgring are not the only German circuits to stage world championship rounds. In 1959 West Berlin's **Avus** circuit staged the German Grand Prix for the one and only time.

Of all the circuits used for world championship races, Avus must rank as the most boring: it was two stretches of autobahn joined together at the ends by two curves, one banked.

Understandably it was fast, and Tony Brooks' winning speed of 146.67mph (236.04kph) was the fastest winning speed in any Grand Prix until 1970. Because of its speed and possible problems to tyres, the race was run in two heats.

Despite its one-off appearance on the world championship calendar, the circuit had been in existence since 1921. Its name is derived from the initials of *Automobil Verkehrs und Ubungs Strasse* (motor traffic and practice road). It staged the inaugural German Grand Prix in 1926.

The two stretches of road ran from Charlottenburg to Nikolasse and were separated by a narrow central strip. The original length was 12.2 miles (19.63km) but in 1937 the north loop banking was made even steeper, which reduced the overall length to 12 miles (19km). After the war the south loop was situated in the Soviet sector of Berlin and a new unbanked loop was added on the now reduced 5.2 miles (8.3km) circuit, which was the one used for the 1959 Grand Prix.

France

The French have regarded their premier race as the 'home' of Grand Prix racing, and why shouldn't they? After all, the first ever race with the title 'Grand Prix' was raced at Le Mans in 1906. Since the formation of the world championship in 1950 the French race has formed part of the championship every year, with the exception of 1955, the year of the Le Mans tragedy.

The **Rheims** circuit was the first to stage a world championship race, and was used eleven times between then and 1966.

A fast circuit, racing first took place at Rheims in 1925 when the Grand Prix de Marne was staged there. Like many famous circuits, its original design utilized public roads. When it was used for the 1950 French Grand Prix it measured 4.856 miles (7.815km) and resembled a triangle, with the Garenne, Thillois and Gueux hairpins forming the three apexes. After an absence of one year, the circuit returned in 1953 but had changed considerably.

It still resembled a triangle but the long downhill straight to the Virage de Thillois was extended. The addition of new pits and facilities made it a much better circuit. Its new length was increased to 5.187 miles (8.347km). The following year the hairpin at Thillois was taken out and a less acute left-hander was added, reducing the length slightly to 5.16 miles (8.302km). The circuit remained unaltered throughout the remainder of its Formula One life, and was last used in 1966 when Jack Brabham won his first championship race for six years; the first win by a driver in his own make of car. After that it lost its status as a top track and was used for Formula Three and Two, and other minor forms of motor sport.

While Rheims was undergoing changes in 1952, the French Grand Prix was held at **Rouen**, a fairly fast circuit laid out in the wooded valley of Les Essarts, just south of Rouen.

A section of the Route Nationale 840 formed part of the circuit at one stage and it originally measured 3.16 miles (4.98km). Rouen was used for the French Grand Prix five times, the last being in 1968, and it offered a variety of tight hairpins and steep uphill and fast downhill curves and bends.

When it appeared on the Grand Prix calendar for the second time in 1957 it had taken on a new appearance. The straight between the Virage de Beauval and Virage du Paradis had disappeared and a whole new top section added, which provided fast corners, long straights and a mixture of uphill and downhill sections. The modified circuit grew to 4.060 miles (6.542km), and

161

remained unaltered during the rest of its time as a Grand Prix circuit.

When the French Grand Prix moved to **Clermont-Ferrand** in 1965 it was the first Formula One race over this circuit. A beautiful course set in the mountains of Auvergne above the town of Clermont-Ferrand in central France, it was constructed in 1958. Known as the Circuit de Charade, it was a hilly circuit that wound its way through the countryside. Its tight bends offered a tough challenge to the drivers. Purported to be built on the rock of an extinct volcano the longest straight was only 650yd (0.594km).

Measuring just over 5 miles (8.055km) in length it had to wait until 1969 before hosting the famous race for a second time. For the 1972 Grand Prix extensive safety work was carried out, and new spectator facilities were constructed. Ironically, after spending all that money it was the last time Clermont-Ferrand was used for a world championship race.

One of the best known names in motor racing is **Le Mans**, home of the world's most famous endurance race. Le Mans has once played host to the French Grand Prix, in 1967; however, the famous Sarthe circuit was not used but the newly built Bugatti circuit. Completed the previous year, it was built as a driving school circuit, and encompassed two car parks. The pits and starting area of the Sarthe Circuit were incorporated but the remainder of the circuit offered little more in character or challenge than several tight corners and a short straight. Hardly surprising it was never used again.

The current home of the French Grand Prix is the **Paul Ricard** circuit built alongside Le Castellet aerodrome 30 miles (48km) east of Marseilles. Finished in 1970 it was built at the request of Paul Ricard, the owner of the famous drinks firm. The main features of the circuit were its high standards of safety and impressive pits area.

The circuit itself is not all that inspiring, largely due to its flat nature, and is not a very popular one with the drivers. The Ligne Droit du Mistral, the back straight, is one of the fastest in the sport, and measures 1.119 miles (1.8km). Speeds of 200mph (321.8kph) are regularly reached on this stretch of the circuit. Its length offers the chance for the faster cars to gain on rivals but it poses the problem to mechanics as to whether the car should be tuned for this stretch of circuit alone, or geared to the bends.

Originally 3.61 miles (5.81km) long the circuit was shortened to its present length of 2.369 miles (3.813km) in 1986 when the section near the Virages de la Sainte-Baume was removed

and a right-hand curve added which reduced the length of the long, back straight. This move followed the death of Elio de Angelis on the straight during a testing session in May 1986. The changes have made the track a better one, and it is now more popular with the drivers. It is also popular as a testing centre for the top Formula One teams.

In the 1970s Paul Ricard shared the French Grand Prix with the **Dijon-Prenois** circuit which was used five times between 1974–84.

A small circuit in eastern France it was built just in time to stage its first Grand Prix in 1974. Small at 2.044 miles (3.289km), it was never regarded as one of the more challenging circuits although it contained a series of twisting uphill and downhill sections. The bends were capable of being taken at around 150mph (241.35kph), but overcrowding was always a problem because it was so small.

The circuit was extended by 558yd (510m) for the 1977 French Grand Prix with the addition of a looped section at the back of the pits which offered three testing bends to the drivers all of which had adverse cambers which posed big problems.

Dijon-Prenois was used for its fifth and final French Grand Prix in 1984, but in 1982 it was used as the venue for the revived Swiss Grand Prix which was won by Keke Rosberg that year, his only success on the way to winning his world title.

Great Britain

Great Britain, along with Italy, has staged a round of every world championship. The most famous of the British circuits, and indeed the home of the first world championship race on 13 May 1950, is **Silverstone**.

Built on a disused airfield near Towcester, Northamptonshire just after the war, Silverstone took over the mantle of Britain's premier motor racing circuit from Brooklands, which suffered its demise at the same time that Silverstone was being created.

The original circuit utilized the runway and perimeter roads of the airfield and measured 3.67 miles (5.9km). A fast circuit, mainly of right-hand bends, the original Grand Prix circuit measured 2.889 miles (4.649km) but was extended to 2.927 miles (4.711km) in 1952, to 2.932 miles (4.719km) in 1975, and to its present-day 2.969 miles (4.778km) in 1987.

Right: An aerial view of Britain's premier circuit, Silverstone.

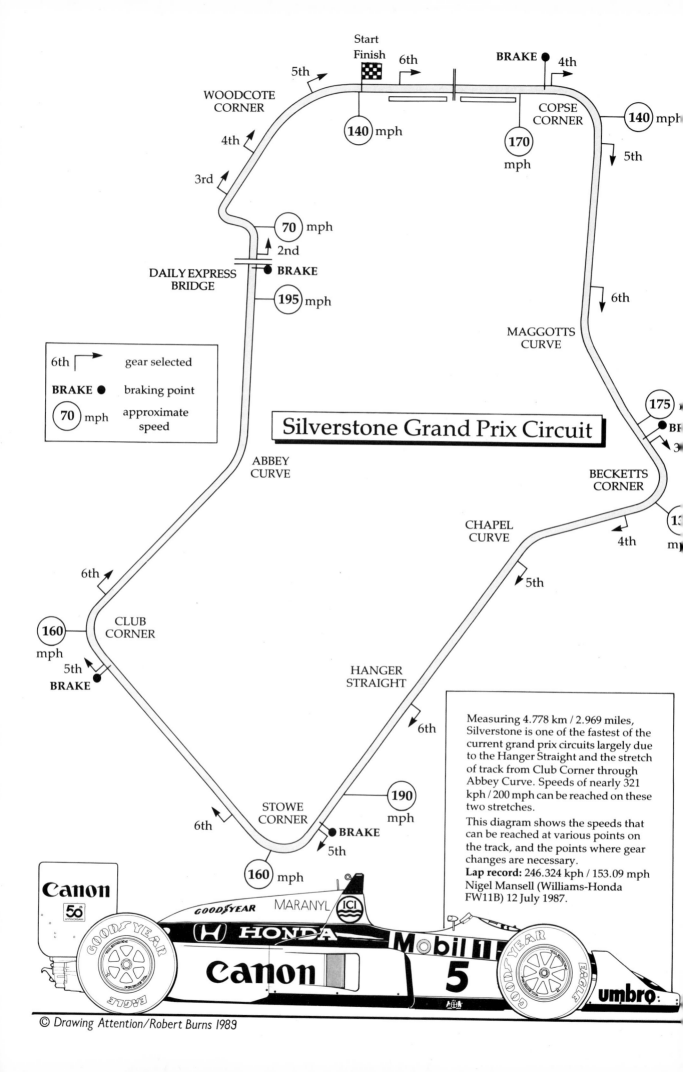

Silverstone Grand Prix Circuit

Start Finish

6th

BRAKE 4th

5th

WOODCOTE CORNER

(140) mph

COPSE CORNER

(170) mph

(140) mph

4th

3rd

5th

(70) mph

2nd

DAILY EXPRESS BRIDGE

BRAKE

6th

(195) mph

MAGGOTTS CURVE

6th → gear selected

BRAKE ● braking point

(70) mph approximate speed

ABBEY CURVE

(175)

BR

BECKETTS CORNER

CHAPEL CURVE

13

m

4th

6th

CLUB CORNER

5th

(160) mph

5th

BRAKE

HANGER STRAIGHT

6th

Measuring 4.778 km / 2.969 miles, Silverstone is one of the fastest of the current grand prix circuits largely due to the Hanger Straight and the stretch of track from Club Corner through Abbey Curve. Speeds of nearly 321 kph / 200 mph can be reached on these two stretches.

This diagram shows the speeds that can be reached at various points on the track, and the points where gear changes are necessary.
Lap record: 246.324 kph / 153.09 mph Nigel Mansell (Williams-Honda FW11B) 12 July 1987.

(190) mph

STOWE CORNER

6th

BRAKE

5th

(160) mph

New pits around Woodcote were responsible for the marginal increase in 1952. The slight increase in 1975 was due to the addition of a chicane at Woodcote which, for safety reasons, slowed down one of the most dramatic bends in motor racing. Further modifications to the Woodcote chicane in 1987 increased the circuit to its present length.

As well as the Grand Prix circuit there is a club circuit and Silverstone has staged all branches of motor sport since its opening in 1948. In 1988 it staged its 22nd British Grand Prix.

Between 1963–87 the British Grand Prix was shared between Silverstone (in odd years) and **Brands Hatch** (in even years). But sadly Brands is no longer on the Grand Prix calendar.

Situated at Farningham, Kent, Brands Hatch was opened in 1949 for Formula Three racing. An undulating course, it offered more variety than the faster Silverstone track. It was a series of one corner after another, and there was little chance of overtaking except along the bottom straight. Paddock bend was one of the most hazardous corners on the circuit.

The first circuit was only 1 mile (1.6km) in length but was extended to 1.24 miles (1.9km) in 1954. The full Grand Prix circuit measured 2.65 miles (4.2km) and was opened in 1960, but it had to wait four years before staging its first British Grand Prix.

Brands was certainly a test of a driver's skill, and its situation offered many fine vantage points for spectators.

Extensive alterations in 1976 saw the completion of a new pit and paddock complex plus alterations to the track itself around the Graham Hill Bend, Cooper Straight and Surtees Bend, all of which meant a slight reduction in lap length to 2.6136 miles (4.2061km)

In addition to staging the British Grand Prix twelve times, Brands staged two other world championship races, the European Grand Prix in 1983 and 1985.

Shortly before it staged the 1986 British Grand Prix the circuit was sold by Eagle Star Holdings to John Foulston in a deal that also gave Foulston control of Oulton Park and Snetterton. However, that 1986 race was the last championship race over the Kent course, despite attempts to get FISA to change its mind and return it to the Grand Prix calendar.

A third British circuit has also staged world championship Grands Prix: between 1955–62 the Liverpool track at **Aintree** was used five times. Well known as the home of the Grand National, the greatest steeplechase in the world, the Aintree motor racing circuit is still in existence and is very popular among club drivers.

The motor racing circuit was laid out in the early 1950s and when it housed the 1955 British Grand Prix one hundred thousand fans turned out to see Stirling Moss beat Juan Manuel Fangio. Motor racing was seen as the financial lifesaver Aintree needed but, as the already high cost of Grand Prix racing spiralled, Aintree could no longer afford to stage such a spectacle and was last used for the British round of the championship in 1962.

The circuit measured exactly 3 miles (4.828km) in length and never changed during its time as a world championship circuit.

Italy

Like Britain, Italy has staged a world championship race every year since 1950. However, it can claim to have staged more races than any other nation because it has, in addition to staging the Italian Grand Prix thirty-eight times, also been the home of the San Marino Grand Prix eight times, making forty-six world championship races in all.

In **Monza** Italy can also claim the most used world championship circuit. It has been the home of no fewer than thirty-seven of the thirty-eight Italian Grands Prix since 1950.

Monza is the fastest of all Grand Prix circuits and Peter Gethin (BRM) won the 1971 Italian Grand Prix at an average speed of 150.75mph (242.62kph) – the only time a Grand Prix has been won at an average speed in excess of 150mph (241kph).

Built in a Royal Park on the outskirts of Milan the Monza autodrome was completed in 1922. A purpose-built banked track, the surrounding roads within the grounds were soon used for racing as well, and they became incorporated within the original circuit. The banked course was demolished in 1933 but a new concrete bowl was constructed in 1955. For many years the banking was considered too dangerous and was the subject of much criticism. And in 1980, for the first time, the Italian round of the world championship was moved from the Autodromo Nazionale di Monza, to Imola, despite Monza improving its safety standards following the tragic death of Ronnie Peterson in 1978.

The length of the championship circuit has varied over the years, due to the many different circuits (11) contained within the Autodromo. The current world championship circuit, however, doesn't take in the banked section anymore, and is 3.604 miles (5.8km) long.

The full circuit has been used several times since 1950 and it provided spectators in the grandstands with the unique feature of seeing

Above: Ayrton Senna in the *John Player* Lotus leads the field in the 1986 British Grand Prix at Brands Hatch.

Left: One of the best-known corners in motor racing, Druids at Brands Hatch.

the drivers pass twice on each circuit. The full circuit has not been used since 1961.

Since then slight modifications have been made regularly to the circuit. Two chicanes, one just past the pits and the other at the Curva del Vialone, were added in 1972 to cut down speeds and reduce slip-streaming. Major changes took place before the 1976 Italian Grand Prix. Chicanes were added to reduce speeds through the Curva Grande and Curva di Lesmo.

This fast circuit has inevitably claimed its toll of lives over the years, notably those of Wolfgang von Trips, Jochen Rindt and Ronnie Peterson.

While Monza took its year off in 1980 the new home of the Italian Grand Prix became **Imola**, set in beautiful countryside near Bologna.

Well-known as a motor cycling circuit from the early 1970s, it had staged a non-championship Formula One race in 1963, won by Jim Clark. But it was in 1979 that it was prepared for world championship Grand Prix racing and in 1980 made its debut.

An anti-clockwise circuit, its tight bends and undulating surface challenges drivers and is hard on brakes. Its three chicanes were designed to slow it down, but it is far from a slow circuit.

Although it has never staged another Italian Grand Prix, Imola is still very much part of the Grand Prix calendar as the home of the San Marino Grand Prix and remains popular with the drivers.

Now measuring 3.132 miles (5.040km) it is slightly longer than its original distance of 3.11

Above: Action from the 1955 Italian Grand Prix at Monza which shows the severity of the banking which has since been removed from this Grand Prix circuit.

Left: The fast Monza circuit has seen many tragedies but none so horrific as that in 1978 when Ronnie Peterson perished in his burning car during the Italian Grand Prix. Despite the efforts of the marshals, James Hunt and Clay Regazzoni, they could not free Peterson.

---

miles (5.00km) following the addition of a further chicane at the Acque Minerali. The circuit is officially called the Circuit Dino Ferrari, named after Enzo Ferrari's late son.

Although Monza and Imola account for every Italian Grand Prix staged since 1950, that is not the end of it as far as Italian world championship circuits are concerned. Italy has hosted one other world championship race: the **Pescara** Grand Prix in 1957.

A road circuit, it had been staging Grands Prix racing since 1924, when Enzo Ferrari had one of his rare successes as a driver. Pescara was added to the world championship rota in 1957 because of the cancellation of the Dutch and Belgian races.

The starting point was just outside Pescara on the Adriatic coast, and the drivers made their way up the Abruzzi mountains to Villa St Maria in the north followed by a fast straight to Monte Silvano before taking a sharp right back to the start. The entire circuit measured a monstrous 15.89 miles (25.579km), the longest course ever used for a world championship race. The huge circuit was not popular and never returned.

United States

The United States has used more different circuits for world championship races than any other nation, a total of eight all in all.

The first US circuit to stage a championship race was the **Indianapolis** raceway in 1950, when the famous 500 mile race formed part of the inaugural world championship. The famous speedway opened in 1910, possibly inspired by the success of Britain's Brooklands circuit. Although simple in design, the original track was made of bricks, not concrete, hence the speedway's nickname, 'The Brickwall'. The last brick to be laid was a golden one. During the 1930s the track was re-surfaced with asphalt.

The circuit is best described as a 'rounded rectangle'. It is 2.5 miles (4.023km) in length with two long straights each measuring 1093yd (1000m) and two short straights each 219yd (200m), all joined by slightly banked corners. As all corners are left-handers, suspension systems are tailored accordingly.

The Indianapolis race was included in the world championship for ten years, and in 1959 the United States staged two championship races for the first time when the **Sebring** circuit staged the United States Grand Prix. The first US Grand Prix for sports cars had been held in 1958 at Riverside, California, but for its Formula One debut it moved to Sebring in Florida.

A converted aerodrome, two runways and perimeter roads formed part of its rather bland 5.2 mile (8.369km) circuit. The first race at Sebring was a six-hour sports car race in 1950.

Bruce McLaren won the 1959 US Grand Prix; the only time Sebring was used for the race. In the 1970s, the circuit fell into disuse when the cost of repairing it outweighed its uses.

When the United States Grand Prix was held again in 1960 it moved to a new home at **Riverside** in California, 60 miles (96km) east of Los Angeles. A major circuit since 1957 it was used for a world championship race on just one occasion, but the race, won by Stirling Moss in a Lotus-Climax, was the last Grand Prix under the old 2½ litre formula.

Because of its lack of financial success at Riverside the US Grand Prix was moved to its third venue in as many years in 1961. This time its new home was **Watkins Glen** overlooking Lake Seneca in New York State. The move to the new circuit was a success, and Watkins Glen remained the permanent home of the US Grand Prix until 1980.

The first circuit was through the streets of the town but following the death of a young fan in 1952 a new purpose-built circuit was con-

Left: Tight corners like this one at Long Beach often produce plenty of action.

Right: The street circuit around Detroit is one of the many American circuits used for Grand Prix racing.

Below: High-rise buildings, tight corners and big crowds were the ingredients for Grand Prix racing at Detroit.

Caesar's Palace on the left and the desert on the right was the setting for the Las Vegas Grand Prix on two occasions.

structed. It originally measured 2.3 miles (3.701km) but was modified extensively, and in 1971 its length was increased to 3.377 miles (5.435km). Not only was an entire new section (The Anvil) added, but also a new pits area.

Despite repairs to the rather bumpy areas of the track in 1980, Watkins Glen was taken off the Grand Prix calendar, and in November 1982 was acquired by the Bank of New York for $1.25 million at a bankruptcy auction. Grand Prix racing has not returned to the once famous circuit although it still plays host to the NASCAR Winston Cup series.

For the first time since 1960, two championship races were held in the United States in 1976 with the inauguration of the United States Grand Prix West. Held every year up to 1983, its home was at **Long Beach**, California. The idea to turn the streets of Long Beach into a racing circuit came from British businessman Chris Pook, who lived in the city. Towards the end of 1975 a circuit had been laid out for a Formula 5000 race, but in 1976 Pook's dreams of staging a championship Formula One race were fulfilled.

With a series of corners, and only one long straight, it was a test of a car's suspension system as much as a driver's concentration.

The first circuit, which took in Ocean Boulevard (the straight), Shoreline Drive and Pine Avenue, measured 2.02 miles (3.251km). In 1982 it was extended slightly and in 1983 a major rebuilding programme took place. It became an even tighter course and the 'bump' at the bottom of Linden Avenue was considered dangerous. The following year, Long Beach was removed from the Formula One calendar; Chris Pook maintained it was too expensive to stage a Grand Prix as opposed to CART racing while FOCA boss Bernie Ecclestone, maintained the reason was because Pook had fallen out with CBS, a much-needed Formula One lifeline. No matter what the reason, Grand Prix racing has not returned to Long Beach.

In 1984 the United States Grand Prix West was replaced by the Dallas Grand Prix, run at **Fir Park**.

A tight, slow, circuit the new surface was very bumpy and was breaking up in places. The close proximity of concrete retaining walls accounted for several crashes during practice, including a broken ankle for Britain's Martin Brundle. Because of the dangers, it looked as though the inaugural Dallas Grand Prix would never take place, but it did . . . only once.

Three years earlier perhaps the most bizarre of all Grand Prix circuits was constructed on the car park of the **Ceasar's Palace** complex in Las Vegas. The home of gambling in the United States, some of the roulette wheels and crap tables were less than 100 yards (91.44m) from the pits area of the racing circuit. The circuit for the newly-instituted Las Vegas Grand Prix in 1981 and 1982, 4½ miles (7.24km) of 10-ton concrete blocks defined the 2.268 miles (3.649km) which consisted of fourteen gruelling turns and just one straight of note. Three months before the flag fell on the first Las Vegas Grand Prix, the 'circuit' was 75 acres of open space!

Remarkably the United States hosted three world championship races in 1982 with the addition of the United States Grand Prix East (later the Detroit Grand Prix). Held through the streets of **Detroit** and based around the $350 million Renaissance Center. Like its more famous counterpart at Monaco, the Detroit circuit used a tunnel as one of its features.

Originally measuring 2.493 miles (4.011km) and a very tight course, two corners were eased slightly in 1983 which extended the circuit to 2.5 miles (4.023km). The circuit certainly doesn't have the appeal of other street circuits, and its uneven surface, tight turns and concrete walls make it a very demanding track for car and driver.

Spain

Spain has been staging Grands Prix since 1913 and was the second country to do so after France. Strangely, the first world championship season did not visit Spain, but since 1951 this country has been part of the championship, albeit erratically.

The first world championship race was held at **Pedralbes** in 1951, one of Barcelona's three circuits, when Juan Manuel Fangio clinched the first of his five world titles. When the championship next came to Spain, three years later, again the 3.936 mile (6.316km) Pedralbes circuit had the honour of staging the race.

The Spanish Grand Prix did not form part of the world championship between 1955–67 and when it returned in 1968 its new home was **Jarama**, 16 miles (25km) north of Madrid. Designed by John Hugenholtz, Jarama was the scene of a major battle during the Spanish Civil War.

Built in a hilly and barren area, Jarama was opened in 1967 when it staged its first International Formula Two race, the Madrid Grand Prix, won by Jim Clark.

An unpopular circuit with the drivers, it was a demanding twisting course with just one long straight and before its first world championship race the GPDA felt the safety standards were lacking. One of their complaints was the safety rails, which were considered to be too high. Ironically, this was the first Grand Prix since Jim Clark's death, which may not have happened had Hockenheim had *any* safety rails . . .

The 2.115 mile (3.404km) circuit was used nine times up to 1980, and in 1981 its size was reduced marginally, but that was to be the last Spanish Grand Prix for five years. When it returned, Jarama was no longer to be its home, that honour went not to Spain's other venue, Montjuich Park, overlooking Barcelona, but to the circuit at Jerez.

Montjuich Park was built in 1933 but fell into disuse after only three years. It was revived in 1966 when it was used for Formula Two racing. However, Montjuich Park eventually received Grand Prix status in 1969 when it staged its first Spanish Grand Prix race.

Made up of public roads, and set in beautiful surroundings, the circuit offered a variety of hairpin bends, fast curves and a short straight which was wide and gave ample opportunity for overtaking.

Its 2.35 miles (3.79km) was used four times between 1969–75 but was then removed as a Grand Prix circuit following complaints about its safety. The current home of the Spanish Grand Prix is the **Jerez** circuit which made its debut in 1986 when Formula One racing returned to Spain after an absence of five years.

Situated in southern Spain near the town famous for its sherry, Jerez was built at a cost of over £5 million. Sadly the claim of it being 'the most modern of Grand Prix circuits' was not received with the same enthusiasm by the drivers when it opened. The trend for clinical safety features and over-tight corners deprived the track of character. Furthermore, it lacked a challenge. Nevertheless the facilities were excellent, and the twisting and undulating circuit was interesting from the spectator's point of view.

A very tight circuit it measures 2.61 miles (4.217km) and has been used every year since making its first appearance.

Canada

Canada did not stage a round of the world championship until 1967 but, with the exception of 1975 and 1987, has staged a round every year since.

Three different circuits have played host to the race, the first being **Mosport Park** near to the shores of Lake Ontario.

The Canadian Grand Prix had been run as a

sports car race since 1961 but, to mark Canada's Centenary in 1967, it was accorded Formula One status and the 2.459 mile (3.957km) Mosport circuit, complete with its ten turns, was honoured with the race.

It was used nine times; by the time the 1977 race came around, it was felt by the drivers to be a long way behind the standards of the European tracks, and it staged its last world championship race.

The new home of the Canadian Grand Prix became the **Ile Notre Dame** circuit along the St Lawrence seaway in Montreal.

Constructed on the site of Expo '67, it was completed in just three months. Measuring 2.796 (4.5km) it was very tight and narrow, and left little or no room for overtaking thus making a good grid position essential.

For its second championship race in 1979 the organizers made modifications by easing the severity of some of the tighter turns and replacing the chicane at the end of the pits-straight with a 'kink'. But once more there was criticism from the drivers ... this time they felt the new 'corner' was too fast and dangerous.

The modified 2.74 mile (4.41km) circuit has remained and is the current home of the Canadian Grand Prix and is one that is now much enjoyed by the drivers because it offers a mixture of a permanent track and a street circuit. It was renamed the **Gilles Villeneuve Circuit** in

memory of the late French-Canadian driver. Coincidentally, Villeneuve won the first world championship race over this circuit in 1978. There was no Canadian Grand Prix in 1987 due to disputes over sponsorship money.

Mont Tremblant-St Jovite is the third Canadain circuit to have been used for a world championship Grand Prix. Located in ski-country north of Montreal it was a very twisty track and staged its first major international event in 1964 when Pedro Rodriguez won in a Ferrari.

Popular in the days of Can-Am, it was the venue for the first ever Can-Am race in 1966, won by Britain's John Surtees. It staged its first world championship Grand Prix two years later.

Belgium

Belgium is another country to have supplied three world championship circuits; the first being the currently-used **Spa-Francorchamps** track.

Situated in the Ardennes, south of Liege, the original track was built in 1924 and its triangular shape measured 8.774 miles (14.117km) but the current circuit bears no resemblance to that. It was completely rebuilt in 1983 and is now 4.312 miles (6.94km) long; the Virage de la Source hairpin, near the start, is one of the few landmarks remaining from the original circuit. Spa is one of the fastest circuits ever to stage Formula

Left: The 1935 Belgian Grand Prix at Spa was not as popular as in recent years. Note also, that apart from a lack of spectators, there is a lack of safety measures.

Previous page: Sparks flying at Spa during the 1986 Belgian Grand Prix.

One racing – only Monza has staged a faster race. However, it became too dangerous in the late 1960s and after staging eighteen championship races in twenty-one years, it was removed from the Grand Prix calendar in 1970. Despite some safety improvements it was still considered too fast and dangerous. It remained in use for sports car races but it was not until after its major re-design in 1983 that it returned as a Grand Prix circuit.

After a year off in 1971 the Belgian Grand Prix returned in 1972 to its new home the **Nivelles-Baulers** circuit 19 miles (30km) south of Brussels.

Much safer than Spa, it was nowhere near as fast, and the organizers made the drivers' safety their number one priority. One long straight, a couple of shorter ones, a large loop and a few curves amply describe the Nivelles circuit. Its length was 2.314 miles (3.724km). Nivelles was used for only two Grands Prix; the second was in 1974.

For political reasons the 1973 race was run at **Zolder**, in Flemish territory. It returned in 1975 and was the permanent home of the Belgian Grand Prix up to 1983 when Spa made its re-appearance.

Known as the Omloop van Zolder (Circuit of Zolder) it was built in the mid-1960s and was used regularly from 1965. Set among sandy hills the undulating course measured 2.6 miles (4.184km)

Portugal

Another country to use three circuits is Portugal with Oporto, Monsanto, and the current home of the Portuguese Grand Prix, Estoril.

The 4.602 miles (7.407km) **Oporto** circuit was used for the inaugural Formula One Portuguese Grand Prix in 1958. The race had been run since 1951, but for sports cars only.

On the outskirts of the city, Oporto was a true street circuit and incorporated all the natural hazards that went with it: kerbs, trees, cobbled streets, lamp posts and even tramlines! An interesting track it had plenty of bends and one fast straight capable of speeds up to 170mph (273kph). The big problem however, was the hundreds of trees around the circuit, which would prove dangerous to any driver skidding off the road.

Oporto staged two championship races, in 1958 and 1960, before the Portuguese Grand Prix was removed from the Formula One calendar. In 1959 the race was run at **Monsanto**, near Lisbon.

Situated in a park adjacent to the Lisbon–Estoril road, the main straight was made up of part of the main road. The 3.38 mile (5.44km) track was used once only.

Grand Prix racing did not return to Portugal until 1984. This time the race had a new permanent home at **Estoril**.

Set among rocky scrubland above the seaside town of Estoril, the 2.6 mile (4.183km) circuit won the approval of the drivers – even if the initial organization left a lot to be desired. Mind you, it was Portugal's first Grand Prix for twenty-four years.

One man who gave the track his seal of approval was Niki Lauda. Runner-up to Alain Prost in the circuit's first race, it was good enough to give him his third world title! The Portuguese Grand Prix and Estoril are now a regular feature of the world championship series each year.

Brazil

Brazil has produced some great drivers over the years and the country's first world championship race coincided with the arrival of their first great champion, Emerson Fittipaldi.

Appropriately, Fittipaldi won the first Brazilian Grand Prix to be accorded championship status in 1973. Its home on that occasion was the twisting **Interlagos** circuit near Sao Paulo.

Interlagos opened in 1940 and was used for various forms of motor racing. To prove its worth as a championship venue it staged a non-championship Formula One race in 1972 and received the seal of approval from the drivers.

Situated on the outskirts of Sao Paulo, the winding and bumpy track offered a tremendous challenge. The Brazilians revelled in the first championship race particularly as local hero Fittipaldi took the chequered flag.

Quite long at 4.946 miles (7.96km) it was used continually until 1977, and then again in 1979 and 1980 when it staged the last of its seven world championship races.

The **Rio de Janeiro** circuit, first used in 1978 and then continually since 1981, is the current home of the Brazilian Grand Prix, traditionally the first race of the season.

A brand new circuit, built on marsh land close to the town of Jacarepagua, 19 miles (30km) south of Rio, it is a tight anti-clockwise layout with a constant stream of bends (some of them quite quick) and only one long straight. Overtaking is a big problem.

Before the race returned in 1981, major repair work had to be carried out because part of the track was sinking. The current circuit now measures 3.126 miles (5.031km).

Left: Estoril, home of the Portuguese Grand Prix since 1984 when the race returned to the Formula One calendar after an absence of 24 years.

Right: Keeping the fans cool at Rio . . . well, it is pretty warm in Brazil in March.

Below: One of motor racing's great sights, the harbour at Monte Carlo.

Above: Inside the tunnel at Monte Carlo.

Left: Monaco, the most famous racing circuit in the world. This is where the million pound cars race alongside the million pound boats.

Japan

Having been involved with Formula One since Honda's days in the 1960s it is, perhaps, surprising to learn that Japan was not used as a stopping-off point for the Formula One circus until 1976. But even then, the Japanese Grand Prix only lasted two years. On both occasions the race was run at the **Fuji International Speedway** situated underneath the extinct volcano, Mount Fuji.

Grand Prix racing had been held in Japan since 1966 but for sports cars or Formula Two only, and the Fuji circuit played host to most of the races.

The circuit measured approximately 9.65 miles (6km) and included a banked section. This part of the course was, however, not used for the Formula One races and the circuit was reduced to 2.709 miles (4.359km). A long, fast straight made up for approximately one third of the total distance. James Hunt finished fourth in the inaugural race, and that was good enough for him to win his world title.

With several teams not attending the 1977 race, the Japanese Grand Prix was removed from the world championship roster. However, it returned in 1987 when the **Suzuka** circuit brought the drama and excitement of Formula One back to the Orient.

Like many newer purpose-built tracks, a feature of the Suzuka is the twisting curves and bends, consequently winning speeds for the 3.641 miles (5.859km) are in the region of 120mph (193kph). It has won the approval of the drivers, and ranks as one of the best of the current Grand Prix circuits.

Monaco

Of all the countries to have provided just one world championship circuit the most famous must surely be the one through the streets of **Monte Carlo**. In fact, it is most probably the best known racing circuit in the world. Monte Carlo is synonymous with motor racing thanks to its famous circuit, and also as the base for the Monte Carlo Rally.

The first Monaco Grand Prix dates to 1929, and when the world championship was launched in 1950, the famous race was an automatic inclusion as one of the seven rounds. It was not included in 1951, and in 1952 the Monaco Grand Prix was for sports cars only. It returned as part of the world championship in 1955 and has remained a permanent fixture ever since.

The Monaco circuit is the shortest on the Grand Prix calendar and between 1955–72 it measured a mere 1.954 miles (3.145km). Since then, following minor changes, it has increased to more than 2 miles (3.218km). The narrow roads twist and turn among the hotels and shops of the Principality. High speeds are impossible and the course is a test of both a driver's concentration, and his car's gearbox.

Monaco lacks a straight as such, and the only chance of building up speed is in the tunnel area and along the harbour wall, although the chicane leading up to the Tabac has been moved in recent years and is now just outside the tunnel exit; designed to slow down the cars before they speed along the harbour area.

No matter how the streets of Monte Carlo change in the future, the Monaco Grand Prix will remain one of the most spectacular of all Grand Prix races.

Mexico

In 1963 Mexico became the second South American country after Argentina to stage a world championship Grand Prix. It was a regular fixture until 1970, and did not return until 1986.

Up to and including the 1988 race, a total of ten Mexican Grands Prix have formed a round of the world championship, and all have been around the dusty **Mexico City** track, built in time for the first non-championship Mexican Grand Prix in 1962.

Situated close to Mexico City's airport and more than 7,000ft (2133m) above sea-level, the big problem that has faced the highly-tuned Formula One cars has been the effect of the altitude on fuel mixtures.

When the *Autodromo Hermanos Rodriguez* (named after the Rodriguez brothers) was used for the revived Brazilian Grand Prix in 1986 the top section containing the hairpin was removed and the first bend changed. The new circuit was nearly a quarter of a mile (400m) shorter than the original circuit.

Australia

'Born' in 1985, the Australian Grand Prix is the second youngest of the current list of world championship Grands Prix. So far, it has been run four times and all races have been at **Adelaide**, a 2.347 mile (3.77km) circuit that winds through the streets of the South Australian capital. Not too tight and not too fast, it is a very popular course and was voted the best organized Grand Prix of the year in its debut season. It now forms the last round of the championship and it was at Adelaide in 1986 that Nigel Mansell bid goodbye to his world championship hopes.

Above: Adelaide, home of the Australian Grand Prix, is one of the newest Formula One circuits.

Right: Another new circuit, the Hungaroring in Budapest, is rated as one of the best circuits in Grand Prix racing.

182

Laid out in the eastern suburbs of the 'City of Churches' the circuit incorporates the city streets and a purpose built section in the Victoria Park horse racing track. Supported and promoted by South Australian premier John Bannon, the Australian Prime Minister Bob Hawke took time off from his busy schedule in 1985 to attend the first Grand Prix.

Hungary

The baby of the Grand Prix circuits is the **Hungaroring** at Mogyórod in Budapest. This twisting and mildy undulating track is 12 miles (19km) north-east of Budapest. Measuring 2.495 miles (4.031km) the drivers regard its twenty corners as demanding a test as Monaco. Used three times so far, the new purpose-built track made its debut in 1986.

Eleven local companies put up £5 million in 1986 and within six months the sparkling new track was completed. The 'Ring' didn't waste any time in gaining in the popularity stakes; it was voted FISA's 'Course of the Year' in 1987 and the drivers were certainly full of praise for it in its inaugural year.

Austria

The second Austrian Grand Prix held in 1964 was the first to receive world championship status and was raced at Zeltweg; the next time the race formed part of the world championship, in 1970, it was run at the Osterreichring which then staged the Austrian Grand Prix continuously to 1987. Sadly there was no Austrian round of the world championship in 1988.

Zeltweg can best be described as 'boring'. Along with Avus and Caesar's Palace it must surely rank as one of the least imaginative of all Grand Prix circuits. It was first used in 1958 when a group of enthusiasts used straw bales to mark out a temporary circuit around the perimeter of the Zeltweg military aerodrome in the Styrian region of Austria.

After staging a couple of Formula Two races in 1959 and 1960 it staged two non-championship Formula One races in the early sixties before getting its first world championship race in 1964. The surface was not suitable for such high-quality racing and it was farewell Zeltweg after just one year.

Following the demise of Zeltweg, the Austrian Automobile Club designed and built the brand new **Osterreichring**, which was completed in 1969.

Set among beautiful pine trees situated near Knittelfeld, and not far from the site of the old

Zeltweg circuit, a feature of the course was the steep climbs, and sharp, fast, descents. It rarely varied from its final length of 3.692 miles (5.942km). An ideal track for spectators, it was one of the most attractive on the Grand Prix circuit at one time.

The narrow pit straight was the scene of chaos at the start of the 1987 Grand Prix and consequently the Osterreichring was not granted a world championship race in 1988.

South Africa

Like Austria, South Africa no longer stages a championship race, but used to be the proud possessor of two championship circuits at East London and Kyalami.

The Prince George road circuit at the holiday resort of **East London** first staged motor racing in 1934. It fell into disuse after the war and it was not until 1960 that it was revived thanks to local enthusiasts. Two years later the South African Grand Prix at East London formed a round of the world championship. It was used again in 1963 and 1965.

The South African Grand Prix dates to 1924 but it was thirty-eight years before it was given world championship status when the 2.436 mile (3.92km) Prince George circuit near Natal was used. The original East London circuit measured nearly 15½ miles (25km).

There was no South African Grand Prix in 1966 but the following year it returned with **Kyalami** as the new venue.

The Johannesburg track was slightly longer than East London at 2½ miles (4.023km) and was used every year (except 1981) between 1968–85.

Opened in 1961, the track replaced the Grand Central Circuit as Johannesburg's top venue and Jim Clark won the first big meeting at Kyalami when he won the Rand Grand Prix in the same year. Situated 5700ft (1738m) above sea level Kyalami was one of the most challenging of all Formula One circuits. It was removed from the Grand Prix list after the 1985 season. Although a reserve for 1986 it was not used.

Holland

Of all the circuits no longer in use, **Zandvoort**, Holland's only world championship circuit, was used more than any other. Between 1952–86 it staged thirty-one world championship races.

Situated among the sand-dunes at the back of Haarlem, the 2.6 mile (4.2km) circuit was devised by enthusiast John Hugenholtz (also responsible for Jarama) and in 1948 the first Zandvoort Grand Prix was staged. Two years later the track was the venue for the first Dutch Grand Prix (non-championship).

Because of its situation, sand blown across the track was the most hazardous problem drivers faced on a course that was not too demanding but offered a great deal of variety: fast corners, tight corners, and long, fast straights.

Over the years the surface deteriorated and after giving the drivers a bumpy ride in 1985 it lost its status as a world championship circuit.

Argentina

Although Argentina was the first South American country to host a world championship race, she can no longer boast such standing, unlike Brazil and Mexico.

Sixteen times between 1953–81 Argentina played host to the Formula One cars and drivers in two distinct periods from 1953–60 and then from 1972–81.

All sixteen championship races were held at the **Buenos Aires Autodrome**, a circuit that

This 1931 cartoon depicts what going to a race meeting was about in that era.

offered ten different combinations of circuits within the autodrome. The Nos. 2, 9 and 15 circuits were used for world championship races. All races up to 1960 were over the 2.431 mile (3.912km) No. 2 circuit.

The circuit, known as 'El Autodrom 17 de Octobre', was opened on 9 March 1952 and had the blessing and encouragement of President Peron. Sadly, the first race in 1953 was marred by a tragedy which saw fifteen spectators killed when Farina's car sped off the track as he desperately tried to avoid a fan who ran out in front of him.

When the Argentine Grand Prix returned after an absence of twelve years in 1972 it was the much improved No. 9 circuit that was used. Slightly smaller at 2.079 miles (3.345km), the building of a new pits area and erection of safety features consistent with modern-day needs made it an impressive circuit.

Another variation of the autodrome was used for the first time in 1974 when the No. 15 circuit was adopted. Much longer than the other two at 3.708 miles (5.968km), it was certainly a lot faster with three fast straight sections. Between then and 1981, when the last Argentine Grand Prix formed part of the world championship, the No. 15 circuit was the race's home.

Sweden

Between 1973–78 the Swedish Grand Prix formed a round of the world championship and all six races were at **Anderstorp**.

A rather flat and uninteresting circuit, it measured 2.5 miles (4km) and used the runway of the disused local airfield as the main straight.

Built in 1968, the Scandinavian Raceway as it was known staged the first Swedish Grand Prix for sixteen years in 1973. The three previous races had all been for sports cars. A popular course, it was unique in that the pits were nowhere near the start!

Switzerland

Switzerland is no longer regarded as a motor racing nation but you may be surprised to learn that the Swiss Grand Prix formed part of the first world championship in 1950. It was only the Le Mans disaster in 1955 that put an end to motor racing in Switzerland (an edict which still exists today) and the country's twenty year association with Grand Prix racing.

Between 1951–54 the five runnings of the Swiss Grand Prix all took place at **Bremgarten**, a tree-lined circuit set in an area of parkland just outside the Swiss capital Berne, and named after the forest through which part of the course ran.

Partly utilizing public roads, and partly private roads, it was first used for motor cycle racing in 1931. It staged its first car race three years later and before the ban on racing in 1955 had been the home of fourteen Swiss Grands Prix. Picturesque, it was a dangerous course with fast bends and very few straights.

A race bearing the title 'Swiss Grand Prix' returned to the championship in 1982 but was raced at Dijon-Prenois in France.

Morocco

... and finally, to the **Ain Diab** circuit, home of the one and only Moroccan Grand Prix to form a round of the world championship.

The 1958 race was the seventh Moroccan Grand Prix but the first to be given world championship status. It had first been held as a tourist car race in 1925 but now it was the turn of the Formula One cars to make their debut around the near-rectangular circuit at Casablanca.

It was over this course that Mike Hawthorn clinched his world championship. After that the Ain Diab circuit was never used for a world championship race again; it was also Mike Hawthorn's last race before his retirement and subsequent untimely death.

7. Tragedies and Ironies

Diavia
AIR CONDITIONERS

S.A.I.
INTERNATIONAL FR

Motor racing is a dangerous sport, and as speeds increased to more than 200mph (321kph) so did the risks. Happily, because of technical advances cars are much safer these days, and the emphasis at racing circuits is very much placed on safety. Consequently, the list of fatalities is dwindling. But over the years some famous names have lost their lives pursuing the sport they love, while others, with the odd twists of fate, have survived the 200mph crashes but then later lost their lives in other circumstances on or off the race track.

One of the best known of such tragedies happened on a Saturday evening in November 1975 when a 6-seater Piper Aztec plane crashed near Barnet in north London. Behind the controls was one of the sport's most successful and likeable characters, Graham Hill.

Having driven in a record 176 Grand Prix races and twice won the world title, Hill had left driving a few months earlier and was concentrating his efforts on developing his own Embassy Formula One team, with the promising youngster Tony Brise as his number one driver. Twenty-three year old Brise signed a two year contract shortly before the accident.

Hill's team had been testing at Paul Ricard. Things had not gone too well and the team returned home a day earlier than planned. They flew from Marseilles on the evening of 29 November but as they approached Elstree airport the area was covered in thick fog. Hill decided to attempt a landing because he had a sound knowledge of the area, but sadly, three miles from the airport, the plane caught two groups of trees and crashed onto Arkley golf course.

Hill was killed instantly, and wiped out with him was his racing team: Brise, team manager Ray Brimble, designer Andy Smallman, and mechanics Terry Richards and Tony Alcock. The team never raced and Graham Hill, who had survived the longest career in Formula One, was never to add to his successes as a team owner.

Lord Snowdon, a close friend of Hill, who worked with him on a campaign to help disabled drivers, should have been on the plane with the team to engage in a photographic session but he cancelled the trip at the last minute.

There was no such luck for ex-drivers Ron Flockhart and Carlos Pace, who also both lost their lives in plane crashes. Edinburgh-born Flockhart obtained a BSc in engineering from his hometown university before getting a job in the textile industry. However he gave it up in 1954 to pursue his first love, motor racing, and he teamed up with BRM.

Scotland's first top driver, 'The Flying Scotsman' as he was known, made his name as a sports car driver, but had a brief flirtation with Formula One in the latter half of the 1950s with BRM, Connaught, Lotus-Climax and Cooper-Climax. His best result was third in the final race of the 1956 season, the Italian Grand Prix at Monza.

But it was in the Jaguar Sports car that Flockhart enjoyed his greatest triumphs. He won Le Mans twice, in 1956 and 1957, first with Ninian Sanderson and then with Ivor Bueb.

In 1962, aged 38, Flockhart still sought adventure, but this time his targets were in the air and not on the race track.

Having held a pilot's licence since 1948 when he learnt to fly a Tiger Moth, he had set his heart on breaking the 24-year-old solo flight record from Melbourne to London. He had previously had one attempt at the record but bad weather and an overheating engine caused him to abandon the attempt at Athens. Now, he was ready for his second attempt.

His plane was a Mustang which he bought from the Royal Australian Air Force. The record attempt was scheduled to start on Monday 16 April 1962, but four days earlier, while testing the plane on a flight from Melbourne to Sydney, it crashed in the Dandenong Range of mountains near Melbourne: Flockhart was killed instantly. His widow, former BOAC hostess Gillian Tatlow, had been Mrs Flockhart for only a few short months.

More recently, the up-and-coming Brazilian driver Carlos Pace also lost his life in an aircraft accident.

In the five years that he had been in Formula One, first with March and then Surtees before becoming an established Brabham driver, Pace earned himself a reputation for being a spectacular driver. He had only one Grand Prix win to his credit at the time of his death, but what a place to enjoy his only win – in front of his home fans in the 1975 Brazilian Grand Prix. Furthermore, the man who followed him home in second place was fellow Brazilian Emerson Fittipaldi, whose brother Wilson was a schoolfriend of Pace's.

The 1977 season started with much promise for Pace and his Brabham BT4. He finished second in the opening round at Buenos Aires and in the South African Grand Prix at Kyalami had taken pole position. Sadly that was to be his last race. Two weeks later he was killed when the light aircraft he was aboard crashed near Sao Paulo. Thirty-two year old Pace was killed immediately. He left a wife and young daughter who shared the loss of a potentially great driver with the rest of the motor racing world.

Previous page: Not all are as lucky as Brian Henton who managed to walk away from this crash in 1981.

Right: After escaping a plunge into the harbour at Monte Carlo four days earlier, twice world champion Alberto Ascari was killed while testing a Ferrari at Monza.

Ironically, that 1977 South African Grand Prix was also the last for another promising driver, Welshman Tom Pryce, killed in one of motor racing's freak accidents.

The most successful Welsh driver since Stuart Lewis-Evans twenty years earlier, Pryce was born in Ruthin, North Wales. The winner of the Grovewood Award in 1973 he showed great potential and made the jump directly from Formula Three to Formula One. He had little difficulty adapting to the sport's *Grande Epreuve* and spent most of his career with the Shadow team.

He made his Grand Prix debut at Nivelles in the 1974 Belgium Grand Prix when he drove the Cosworth powered Token RJ02, a British made kit-car. When he made his next appearance, at Zandvoort six weeks later, he was in the DN3 Shadow.

Although he never won a Grand Prix he did win the 1975 Formula One Race of Champions at Brands Hatch. His best world championship result was third in the 1975 Austrian Grand Prix.

With the 1977 championship only two races old, the third round moved from South America to South Africa. The 23rd South African Grand Prix took place on 5 March. The drama started on lap 22 when Pryce's Shadow team-mate Renzo Zorzi came to a halt after a fuel pipe broke and the leaking fuel caught fire. On the opposite side of the track two marshals were waiting to cross to tend to Zorzi's car. When they made the dash, Hans Stuck and Tom Pryce had just started their 23rd lap and were approaching the brow of a hill which hid the marshals. As they came over the brow it was impossible for the two drivers to take evasive action. One of the marshals scampered clear. The other was hit by Pryce's car.

The marshal, Jansen van Vuuren, a 19-year-old reservations clerk at Johannesburg's Jan

Smuts airport, was killed instantly. The large fire extinguisher he was carrying flew straight into Pryce's face, killing the Welshman immediately. His car continued uncontrollably at around 160mph (257kph) with the accelerator on full throttle. As the car approached the Crowthorne corner Jacques Laffite pulled level ready to overtake, unaware of what had happened. Pryce's car then veered off the track and into the catch-fencing, taking Laffite's Ligier with it. Laffite was safe, but Pryce was dead. Ironically, the fire in Zorzi's car was only a minor one. Remarkably, it was fifty years and two days to the date when another great Welsh driver, J. G. Parry Thomas, was killed on Pendine Sands.

After his death, Pryce's wife of two years, Nella, and Tony Brise's wife Janet, who both shared the misery of losing their husbands in tragic circumstances, formed a partnership and opened an antique shop in Fulham.

One of the saddest disasters motor racing has known occurred on Sunday 7 April 1968 when Jim Clark, the greatest driver of his era, was killed at Hockenheim in West Germany.

After surviving many scares in his early Formula One days he became invincible. It is therefore ironic that the greatest Grand Prix driver should lose his life in a Formula Two race.

Because of Lotus's relationship with Ford, Colin Chapman released his star driver for other engagements when the Lotus team's programme permitted. On the weekend of Clark's death Ford wanted the Scot to drive their new 3 litre prototype sports car in the BOAC International 500 at Brands Hatch, but Chapman wanted Clark to drive the Lotus in the Deutschland Trophae Formula Two race around the pine forests at Hockenheim. The arguments raged until it was eventually decided that Clark should race in Germany.

The race was scheduled for 20 laps of the fast Hockenheim circuit. It was Clark's first drive over the famous circuit and he was far from happy from the start. On the 6th lap he was struggling in 8th place in his Lotus-Cosworth. Suddenly, coming out of a gentle right-hander he inexplicably lost control of his car. It careered down the track for about 500 yards (457m) before somersaulting and crashing into some of the many trees that were waiting for the wayward car. There was no protection from Armco barriers at Hockenheim in those days.

Clark's car disintegrated immediately and debris was spread over a vast area. He was rushed to the Heidelberg University Hospital but massive internal injuries, a broken neck and a skull fracture resulted in Jim Clark being pronounced dead on arrival.

The cause of the accident was never known and a question that was asked for many years afterwards was how could such a great driver die in such circumstances?

Clark's accident happened out of view of the eighty thousand fans. When the announcement was made there was a stunned silence, a typical reaction of motor racing people the world over when they hear of a death of a driver.

Would it have been a different story if he had driven that prototype Ford at Brands Hatch?

One of the first greats of world championship racing, Alberto Ascari, also lost his life on the track. The tragedy of Ascari's death is that four days earlier he survived what could also have been a fatal accident.

Ascari had motor racing running through his blood and from a very early age wanted to emulate his father, Antonio, and become a racing driver. Despite losing his father when he was only 6 years of age, the young Alberto still wanted to follow in his footsteps.

When the world championship started in 1950 it was soon realized that Ascari and his Ferrari would be a force to be reckoned with and in 1953 Ascari became the first man to win successive world titles when his Formula Two Ferrari 500 was the outstanding car of the age.

He missed much of the 1954 season with the troubled Lancia team. Their Grand Prix car took a while to get ready, but he raced for them in sports car races and won that year's Mille Miglia. His Lancia D50 was ready for the start of the 1955 season but after 22 laps of the opening race at Buenos Aires he skidded out of the race. In the next race, the Monaco Grand Prix, he was involved in the first of two inexplicable accidents within four days, the second of which was to claim his life.

At Monte Carlo he was on the 81st of the 100-lap race. Lying second to Stirling Moss at the time, he approached the tunnel. When he came out of the tunnel he found himself in the lead after Moss's car blew its engine. Then, suddenly, Ascari made a mistake at the chicane. His car slid across the road, into the straw bales and over the harbour wall. The large crowd held its breath. Happily Ascari emerged and swam to a rescue boat. Shaken, his only injury was a broken nose.

At Monza four days later, while testing a borrowed 3 litre Ferrari sports car from his friend Eugenio Castelotti, which Ascari intended racing the following weekend, his luck finally ran out.

At 1pm on 26 May 1955, the Ferrari left the Monza track just after the Lesmo bend. He was not travelling very fast at the time as the car

Above: All that remained of Jo Siffert's BRM after his tragic accident in 1971.

Right: Jo Siffert in his familiar Swiss national helmet.

skidded and turned over several times, killing Ascari outright from severe head and chest injuries. The accident was a mystery, and like Jim Clark's accident thirteen years later the question asked was: 'How could it happen to such a great driver?' Also, for some unknown reason, Ascari was not wearing a crash helmet that fateful day at Monza.

When Antonio Ascari lost his life after his Alfa Romeo overturned during the 1925 French Grand Prix at Montlhéry he was aged 36 and left a widow with two young children. Alberto Ascari was also 36 when he was killed. He also left a widow with two young children.

So many drivers have lost their lives satisfying their search for excitement around the racing circuit that it would be impossible to recall them all. The ones chosen here are those that have the 'what-would-have-happened-if' element to them. And that is exactly the question that could have been asked following the death of Swiss driver Jo Siffert in 1971: 'What would have happened if the Mexican Grand Prix had not been cancelled?'

Due to safety work being carried out to the Mexico City circuit the final race of the 1971 season was cancelled. In its place there was the Rothmans World Championship Victory Race at Brands Hatch held to honour Jackie Stewart's recently won world championship success.

Siffert was the BRM team leader, a role he assumed following the death of Pedro Rodriguez during a sports car race at the Norisring in Germany earlier in the season. Siffert, who had been in Formula One since 1962, had just completed his most successful season, finishing 5th in the world championship. In the last race of the season at Watkins Glen he came second to François Cevert.

At Brands on that fateful day Siffert occupied pole position for the 40 lap race. As he braked going into Hawthorn on the 15th lap bits started flying off his BRM. The car shot off the track and into the left-hand bank before bouncing upside down onto the track. It burst into flames in front of the approaching John Surtees. Fireman couldn't get near as the fuel tanks exploded and Siffert perished in his car. The race was immediately cancelled and Siffert's BRM team-mate Peter Gethin was declared the winner.

A former Swiss 350cc motor cycling champion, Siffert once rode in the Isle of Man TT. He was a great sports car driver but was reaching his peak in Formula One. Sadly, the true potential of Jo Siffert was never seen. For BRM it was a double tragedy because they lost their two top drivers in one season.

As we have seen, Ron Flockhart lost his life

pursuing a new challenge; Frenchman Didier Pironi was to suffer the same fate, but at the wheel of his powerboat rather than an aeroplane.

A Formula One driver since joining Tyrrell in 1978, Pironi survived an horrific accident in 1982 which ended his Grand Prix career. Five years later he was not to be so lucky when he was involved in an accident in the Needles Trophy powerboat race off the Isle of Wight.

Pironi spent his last year in Grand Prix racing with the Ferrari team. His team-mate was the French-Canadian Gilles Villeneuve and the two men got on well until the 1982 San Marino Grand Prix.

Contrary to team instructions Pironi overtook his team-mate to take the chequered flag, with Villeneuve second. After that the two men hardly spoke again. Thirteen days later the Canadian was dead following an accident during practice at Zolder. After a succession of good results Pironi got himself into the lead in the race for the world drivers' championship. But his dream of lifting the world title ended at Hockenheim during the German Grand Prix. Following a bad accident he was trapped in his car for nearly an hour as he was cut free. His legs were shattered; thirty operations later he still hadn't regained full movement of his right leg.

Forced to give up motor racing he switched his interest to the thrill of powerboat racing but on 23 August 1987 he was killed when his craft was involved in a accident. French TV broadcaster Bernard Giroux and Ligier Formula One engineer Jean-Claude Guernard also lost their lives.

Shortly before the tragic accident, 35-year-old Pironi was told by his girlfriend Catherine Gouz that she was expecting their first child, after many years of trying to start a family. Conceived by the test tube method adopted by Patrick Steptoe, Catherine gave birth to twin boys six months later. She called the first Didier and the second was named after Gilles Villeneuve. Sadly, Pironi never survived to see his two sons.

The ultimate irony for any racing driver who risks losing his life after flirting with danger and speed on the race track must be to die as a result of a car accident on a normal road. But that fate has befallen several men over the years.

Perhaps the most famous car accident involving a Grand Prix driver was in January 1959 when the ebullient Mike Hawthorn was killed only months after retiring from racing as the reigning world champion.

Following the death of his friend Peter Collins at the Nurburgring in 1958, Hawthorn left racing

at the end of that season, with the added bonus of capturing the world title from Stirling Moss in the last race of the season. When he left he commented: 'I have been a racing motorist for eight years. I got to the top; I became world champion. I decided now is the time.'

After retiring, Hawthorn continued to run the family garage at Farnham with his mother. His father Leslie had been killed in a car accident while returning from a race meeting at Goodwood in 1954. Hawthorn had also started a new career writing about motor racing and motor races.

Sadly the full potential of his new career was never realized because, on his way to a luncheon appointment in London Hawthorn was killed when his 3.4 litre Jaguar was involved in a collision with a lorry on the Guildford by-pass.

The accident happened on a long straight stretch of road which was slightly wet after recent rain. Hawthorn had just passed his friend and fellow racing driver Rob Walker. The next minute Walker saw Hawthorn's Jaguar leave the road.

After accelerating up the straight the car suddenly skidded and caught the rear end of a heavily-laden lorry coming the other way. The Jaguar careered across the road, over the kerb,

Above: Didier Pironi in the Ligier JS11A. After surviving an horrific accident at Hockenheim he left racing. Sadly, he was killed in 1987 pursuing his new 'love', powerboat racing.

Below: The remains of Mike Hawthorn's car after his tragic accident in 1959.

and nearly uprooted a small tree. A doctor who had been filling his car with petrol at a filling station 200 yards (182m) up the road was quickly on the scene but there was nothing that could be done. Hawthorn was dead before the ambulance arrived.

The subsequent inquest recorded an accidental death verdict on 29-year-old Hawthorn. Ironically, the world champion could have been driving in the Monte Carlo Rally at the time. He was offered a drive as Les Leston's co-driver but turned it down because he felt the race was too dangerous.

Another world champion to lose his life on the open road was Dr Giuseppe Farina, the first champion in 1950.

A doctor in political science, his love of motor racing was greater than any academic affiliation he might have had. He started racing Maseratis before the war. After the hostilities he drove for Alfa Romeo before falling out with them, but they healed their rift in time for the first world championship season. Farina won three of the six European championship rounds and took the inaugural title by three points from Juan Manuel Fangio.

A series of accidents, including the one in the disastrous 1953 Argentine Grand Prix when fifteen people were killed, and the 1954 Mille Miglia when his car burst into flames, caused Farina eventually to announce his retirement midway through the 1955 season.

Although he quit the European Grand Prix scene, he still had two attempts at the Indianapolis 500 in 1956 and 1957, but each time failed to qualify. After the death of his reserve driver Keith Andrews while testing Farina's car before the qualifying sessions for the 1957 race, Farina made the decision to make a complete break from racing.

With his racing days over Farina concentrated on his business as a Jaguar and Alfa Romeo distributor. He was also involved in the family Pininfarina coachbuilding business. He still kept a watch on the racing scene and in 1966, while on his way to the French Grand Prix at Rheims, he was killed when he lost control of his Lotus-Cortina near Aiguebelle in the French Alps. 'Nino' Farina was aged 60 at the time and the man who had escaped numerous crashes during his twenty-two-year racing career was powerless to do anything about this latest skirmish as

Left: The showman Mike Hawthorn (right) sharing a joke with Stirling Moss at Silverstone in July 1958. Six months later the fun-loving Hawthorn was dead.

Above right: One of the greatest world motor cycling champions, Mike Hailwood. He won nine world titles between 1961–67.

Right: Mike Hailwood in his Lotus 25 at the 1964 Monaco Grand Prix where he picked up his first world championship point for finishing 6th.

Left: The first world champion Giuseppe Farina, seen here after winning the International Trophy at Silverstone in 1950. It was ironic that after surviving in one of the most dangerous of sports, he should lose his life on the open roads in the French Alps.

Right: A world champion on two wheels, and also a top class racing driver, Mike Hailwood lost his life on his way to a chip shop.

Next page: The Portuguese Grand Prix of 1984 was a 1st and 2nd for the McLaren pair of Prost and Lauda but in 3rd place was Brazilian Ayrton Senna in his Toleman showing that he was a driver to be reckoned with in the future.

his car skidded off the road and into a telegraph pole.

Giuseppe Farina was an enigma. Despite being world champion he refused to let the press get inside his private life and little was known about the man away from the race track. On the track, however, he was one of the first greats and was said to drive as if 'the devils were behind him and the angels ahead of him'. Unfortunately, there was no angel in front of him that June day in 1966 high up in the French Alps.

Had Farina reached his destination in 1966 then he would have witnessed the Grand Prix debut of Britain's Mike Parkes, elevated to the Ferrari team after John Surtees terminated his contract. Coincidentally, Parkes, like Farina, was to lose his life in a car accident.

Remarkably, along with team-leader Lorenzo Bandini, Parkes started the race from the front row of the grid (the third place was occupied by ex-Ferrari man Surtees, now with Cooper). The success story was so nearly complete as Parkes was beaten to the chequered flag only by Jack

Brabham. He had three more races that season and finished second again at Monza. A bright future was being predicted for the Englishman.

However, in the second race of the next season, at Spa, his Ferrari crashed heavily after sliding on some oil. The car overturned and Parkes was thrown out. His leg was badly damaged, and after two years in hospital his racing career was over.

The great career that Mike Parkes promised was never seen. He gave glimpses of brilliance during his brief time in Formula One and behind the wheel of the Ferrari sports car he showed his skill in winning the Sebring 12-Hour race in 1964.

Educated at Haileybury where Stirling Moss was two years his elder, Parkes left school for an apprenticeship at Rootes' Coventry factory. He was later to work on the design of the Hillman Imp but left before its launch to take up a job in the Ferrari factory. A dedicated engineer he became equally proficient behind the wheel when offered his first drive with them in the early 1960s.

ning on the Isle of Man before eventually hanging up his leathers.

On Saturday evening 21 March 1981, Mike, daugher Michelle (9) and son David (6) were travelling in Hailwood's 3½ litre Rover along the A435 at Portway, near the Warwickshire–Worcestershire border, when they were in a collision with a lorry which tried to go through a gap in the dual carriageway. Hailwood's car went into the tailgate and Michelle was killed instantly. David was allowed out of the Birmingham Accident Hospital the following day, but Hailwood received serious head injuries. His life hung in the balance until 3.16 pm on the Monday afternoon when he was pronounced dead. His actress-wife Pauline was at his bedside.

Mike Hailwood had endured a disaster-free motor cycling career, with the exception of the odd skirmish. In Grand Prix racing he was awarded the George Medal for bravery after pulling Clay Regazzoni from his blazing car during the 1973 South African Grand Prix. A year later, Hailwood suffered the worst of his Grand Prix crashes when he had to be cut free from his McLaren after a bad accident on the 13th lap of the German Grand Prix at the Nurburgring. That accident brought about the end to his car racing career. The accident on the A435 in March 1981 brought about the end of a great life.

Finally, one cannot recall such sad moments without mentioning the tragic end to the brave Swedish driver Gunnar Nilsson, who lost his nine-month battle against cancer in October 1978.

He had been in Formula One for a mere two seasons and in his thirty-one races had just one win at Zolder in the JPS Lotus 78. The top newcomer of 1976 he soon became one of the most popular men on the Grand Prix circuit.

After two seasons with Lotus, Gunnar switched to the new Arrows team for the 1978 season, but he never took up the contract because he learnt he had terminal cancer.

Days before his eventual death on Friday 20 October 1978, he launched his Gunnar Nilsson Cancer Treatment appeal. He refused pain killing drugs in order to spend his last days sending out letters to his many friends in motor racing and show business, appealing for funds for the Charing Cross Hospital, where he had been treated. He even made telephone calls to fellow Swedes Bjorn Borg and the pop group Abba, seeking their help in getting the campaign off the ground. The ex-submarine radio officer from Halsingborg eventually lost his battle just a month before his 30th birthday as yet again another motor racing favourite was taken away from the sport in tragic circumstances.

After his bad accident Parkes remained in Italy where his services as a consultant engineer were much sought after. Tragically, on 29 August 1977 he was killed when his car was involved in a collision with a lorry near Turin to make 1977 a bleak year for motor racing.

Four years later, in 1981, one of motor sport's all-time greats Mike Hailwood was also to lose his life in tragic circumstances, and in an accident well away from the racing arenas of the Isle of Man, Silverstone or Brands Hatch. He was killed on the outskirts of Birmingham while taking his two children for a fish and chip supper. Sadly, his daughter Michelle was also killed.

Winner of nine world motor cycle titles and fourteen Isle of Man TT races, Hailwood first tried his hand at Formula One racing in 1963 but with little success. He concentrated on car racing full time in 1967 and after enjoying success at Formula 5000 he made a return to Grand Prix racing. His best result was in the 1972 Italian Grand Prix when he finished 2nd to Emerson Fittipaldi.

He returned to bike racing and carried on win-

8. Great Races

The roar of the engine and the sight of a Grand Prix car racing around the track at more than 100mph is dramatic enough; add to it the precision and skill of the driver and the chess-like confrontations as one racer attempts to outwit the other and motor racing offers all that is exciting in sport. If, on top of all that, a race can include the added ingredient of a tense battle right up to the chequered flag then there is little to beat motor racing as the most spectacular of all sports.

Every motor race is exciting. But we have dug into the archives and come up with some truly memorable races that epitomise all that is great in Formula One racing.

It is perhaps fitting that the first great race we recall is the **1953 French Grand Prix** because it was the French who staged the first ever Grand Prix in 1906.

By the time Rheims staged the 30th French Grand Prix in 1953 world championship racing was three years old. The Italians (Farina, Fagioli, Ascari and Taruffi) and the Argentinians (Fangio and Gonzalez) had dominated the championship, but now their hold was to be broken by a genial Englishman.

The British challenge of Reg Parnell, Peter Whitehead and Ken Wharton never materialized in the early championship years, but in 1952 the fun-loving Mike Hawthorn arrived on the scene in his Cooper-Bristol. He picked up points in three championship races, including a 3rd place in the British Grand Prix at Silverstone.

Hawthorn teamed up with Ferrari for the 1953 season and in his first race, the Argentine Grand Prix, finished a creditable 4th. He followed that with top-six placings in the Dutch and Belgian Grands Prix before arriving in France for the French race.

For the first time since the 1930s, Britain had a driver capable of breaking the domination of the top European, and now Argentinian, drivers. There was no doubt Hawthorn had a car capable of winning, particularly as the championship was run to Formula Two rules. His Ferrari 500 was the most reliable Grand Prix car at the time.

The Maseratis of Fangio and Gonzalez offered a threat to the European charge but with men like Ascari, Farina and Villoresi beside Hawthorn at Rheims, the Ferrari team was certainly the strongest. But which one of the strong team would take the chequered flag? If it was down to Fangio and Gonzalez the answer would be none of them.

Only 1.3 seconds separated the first six cars on the grid after practice, and the four-car front row of the grid was occupied by the two Argentinians and the Ferrari pair of Ascari and Hawthorn. Ascari was fastest in practice. The Ferrari team, however, nearly pulled out of the race.

A sports car race preceded the Grand Prix and the Ferrari, driven by Maglioli and Carini, was disqualified for technical infringements. As a result, Ferrari was prepared to withdraw its Grand Prix team, but eleventh hour discussions stopped their withdrawal and they were all set for Rheims.

Gonzalez in his Maserati sped away from the start and his decision to start the race with a half full fuel tank appeared to be paying dividends. After 25 of the 60 laps he still led and had built up a 20-second lead. Behind him it was a battle for second place between Ascari, Hawthorn, Fangio, Farina and Villoresi. Those five had constantly been changing places as they took it in turns to pursue the Argentinian leader.

Fangio, as always, kept a careful eye on the activities in the pits and knew that his teammate was due for his re-fuelling stop. Fangio cleverly worked his way into second position and while Gonzalez was re-fuelling he took the lead.

When Gonzalez re-joined the race the pace had hotted up so much that he was back in 6th place, despite his one-time big lead. During the activity of Gonzalez's pit stop, it was Hawthorn who took up the challenge to chase Fangio. Gradually these two pulled away and it was a Ferrari versus Maserati battle for more than 150 miles (241km).

The lead constantly changed hands. Fangio had the advantage on the long straight leading to Thillois but on the two hairpins Hawthorn fully utilized the better acceleration of the Ferrari out of the bends.

Behind the two leaders there was another great struggle going on as Gonzalez attempted to regain his position at the front of the pack while Ascari and Farina battled for third place putting great pressure on the two leaders.

As Fangio and Hawthorn came down the finishing straight to start the penultimate lap they were level as were Gonzalez and Ascari only a second behind. The situation hardly changed as all four drivers started the 60th and final lap. Hawthorn was marginally ahead of Fangio but the Englishman was up against the skill and experience of the Argentinian as they approached the last 5 miles (8.347km). In his favour, the 24-year-old Hawthorn had a daring approach and a desire to win.

All four cars were neck-and-neck on the final lap. As they approached the final hairpin at Thillois it was the Englishman who had his nose in front. Fangio made a slight mistake by sliding

the tail of his car. Hawthorn used the Ferrari's power to pull away and after nearly three hours of racing crossed the line 45 yards (40 metres) ahead of his rival, with Gonzalez third and Ascari fourth.

Mike Hawthorn became the first Englishman to win a world championship Grand Prix, and the large crowd at Rheims that day were privileged to witness one of the greatest and closest Grands Prix ever. Among the starters that day was Stirling Moss. Two years later Moss had the honour of becoming the second Briton to win a Grand Prix when he won the British Grand Prix at Aintree.

Four years after the great race at Rheims Juan Manuel Fangio was involved in another Grand Prix classic, but this time he was a winner.

The venue was the Nurburgring on a hot August day; the race the **1957 German Grand Prix** and Fangio needed a victory for his fourth consecutive world title, and fifth in all.

Having won three of the four rounds of the championship (excluding Indianapolis) there was an air of inevitability about the great man's presence behind the wheel of his Maserati 250F. After all, his record was second to none: four world championships and 22 Grand Prix wins, a total that was nine more than his nearest rival Ascari.

However, engine trouble just after half way in the previous championship race, at Aintree, indicated Maserati was beginning to falter, particularly as all five had to pull out of the Aintree race with one problem or another.

The practice session at the Nurburgring, however, did nothing to cause alarm among the Maserati ranks as both Fangio and Jean Behra took their places on the front row of the four-car grid, with the Argentinian in pole position.

Above: With Mike Hawthorn already over the finishing line as the first British winner of a world championship race, the race for second place continued between the two Maserati drivers Fangio (18) and Gonzalez (20). Fangio won.

The early pace was set by the other two front row occupants, Hawthorn and Peter Collins. Both were in Lancia-Ferraris and were running the race without any stops for fuel or tyres. Fangio hung on the tail of third man Collins until cleverly working his way to the front on the 3rd lap of the 22-lap race.

At the half-way stage Fangio had built up a 30-second lead. The only two men offering a challenge were Hawthorn and Collins but Fangio still had to come into the pits for fuel and tyres. His mechanics took nearly one-and-a-half minutes to carry out the work and his half-a-minute lead suddenly became a 50-second deficit.

The true test of Fangio's skill and of his car's ability were about to be witnessed as he tried to pull back the deficit with 10 laps of the monster circuit to go.

It was only after the new tyres bedded in and the fuel load lightened that Fangio started to make an impression on the two Englishmen. He had reduced the lead to about 30 seconds after lap 16. Despite pleas from the Ferrari pit men to go faster, Collins and Hawthorn could not prevent Fangio's burst as lap-after-lap he set new records until lap 20 when he reduced the lap record by 11 seconds as he covered the 14.17-mile (22.81km) circuit in 9min 17.4sec at an average of 91.518mph (147.252kph). With two laps to go Fangio had reduced the gap to two seconds.

On the penultimate lap he took second place when he went past Collins on the third bend, the Nurdkurve. And then halfway round the 21st lap he went past Hawthorn to recapture the lead he lost when he went into the pits. The great Argentine driver never lost the lead again and crossed the finishing line 3.6 seconds ahead of Hawthorn.

The 200,000 fans who lined the tree-clad circuit in the Eifel Mountains were treated to one of the greatest individual displays of driving as Fangio won the 23rd and last Grand Prix of his career, a win that assured him of his fifth world title.

Mike Hawthorn has figured in both selected great races so far; he also played a prominent role in the third race, the **1958 Moroccan Grand Prix**.

This race has only once been included in the world championship calendar, but its sole appearance played a crucial role in deciding the outcome of the 1958 drivers' championship.

When Fangio retired mid-way through the 1958 season the way was paved for Moss to win the title that had eluded him for so long. Standing in his way now, however, was Mike Hawthorn, the first British winner of a world championship Grand Prix five years earlier.

The Grand Prix circus made its way from Monza to Casablanca for the eleventh and final round of the championship. The scales were heavily tipped in Hawthorn's favour who started the race with 40 points to Moss's 32. Moss had to win and also register the fastest lap (worth an extra point in those days); second place was no good to him. And if Hawthorn finished 1st or 2nd, or 3rd and set the fastest lap then he would take the title, irrespective of what Moss did.

Hawthorn was still with Ferrari and driving the Dino 256, while Moss had switched from Cooper to Vanwall.

All the drivers were presented to the Moroccan King before the start as Moss and Hawthorn lined up in first and second places on the grid.

Moss leapt off from the start and despite a challenge from Hawthorn's Ferrari team-mate, Phil Hill, the Englishman could not be caught. Hawthorn had been second at one stage but by lap 13 was down to fourth place; that was no good to him, he had to finish 1st or 2nd to win the title. It was at this stage that Moss nearly threw away his chance when he clipped Seidel's Maserati on lap 16. Fortunately, it was Seidel who was forced out of the race and not Moss.

After 21 of the 53 laps Moss was approximately 15 seconds ahead of Phil Hill who was well ahead of team-mate Hawthorn who had moved into third place. Hawthorn needed that second place and the message came from the pits for

Hill to move over and let Hawthorn overtake. There was no chance of Hawthorn winning the race, but if he could pass Hill and stay in second place then the world title would be his.

Moss was aware of the situation but was powerless to do anything about it. His only chance was for *his* team-mate Stuart Lewis-Evans to finish ahead of Hawthorn but on lap 42 the engine on Lewis-Evans's Vanwall blew up. And as his car careered off the track to apparent safety it caught fire. Lewis-Evans leapt out of the car in flames. Tragically, he died six days later as a result of his burns.

That was the end of Moss's championship ambitions. He won the race by 1 min 24 secs and also set the fastest lap for a maximum nine points, but the title went to Mike Hawthorn by a solitary point. The Morocco Grand Prix may have only once been included in the world championship, but what a significant, and sad, race it turned out to be. Moss never came that close to winning the world title again.

For close finishes in 'back-to-back' races, the **1961 Dutch and Belgian Grands Prix** are unparalleled. And in both races the central characters were the Ferrari duo of Wolfgang von Trips and Phil Hill.

The Dutch Grand Prix was the second round of the 1961 championship. First blood had gone to Stirling Moss in his Lotus-Climax at Monaco who was followed home by two Ferraris. Now it was Ferrari's turn to turn the tables.

The three Ferraris of Hill, von Trips and Richie Ginther occupied the front row of the grid on a bright day at Zandvoort, and it was von Trips and Hill who dominated the race from the start. The German led from flag to flag, and apart from a brief spell on lap 17, when Jim Clark took second place, he was followed by the American Hill. Clark continued to try and claw back von Trips but the Ferrari proved too good for the Lotus. In the end it was Hill who made a charge at his team-mate but von Trips held on to take the chequered flag by a mere 0.9sec.

Apart from showing the worth of the Ferraris, the race was notable for the fact that all fifteen starters were running at the end, there had been no retirements. Furthermore, none of the fifteen cars made a pit-stop, something unique in the history of Formula One racing.

Von Trips and Hill were to share the spoils in the next race at Spa three weeks later. This time the honours went to Hill with von Trips in second place. But again less than one second separated the two men.

Ferrari occupied the front row of the grid. By lap 4 the Ferrari domination showed as they pulled away from the rest of the field. With five laps

The 1930s was a great era for motor racing and the Nurburgring one of the sport's best-known venues.

203

remaining only eight cars were on the same lap – four of them were Ferraris. Ginther and Olivier Gendebien had been having a private duel for 3rd place which Ginther won by 26 seconds but the real race was for 1st place as Hill gained revenge for Zandvoort by crossing the line 0.7 seconds ahead of his team-mate, ²⁄₁₀ths of a second less than the winning margin three weeks earlier.

The two men were closely to contest the championship that season, and indeed they finished the season in 1st and 2nd places. But sadly, von Trips never saw the season out; he lost his life at Monza.

For keeping the fans guessing as to who will be the new world champion until the very last race of the season, the 1958 Moroccan Grand Prix can be outdone by the **1964 Mexican Grand Prix** which went to the very last lap of the season before deciding the world champion.

As the drivers arrived in Mexico City for the tenth and final race of the season the drivers' championship read:

1. Graham Hill   (Great Britain)
   BRM   39 points
2. John Surtees   (Great Britain)
   Ferrari   34 points
3. Jim Clark   (Great Britain)
   Lotus   30 points

Hill needed to come 1st or 2nd to guarantee the title, but after that it depended on where Surtees finished. Clark could win the title but he had to win the race and Hill finish out of the points. Hill started as favourite, particularly as he had won the previous round at Watkins Glen. But John Surtees was keen to add the world drivers' title to the seven motor cycling world titles he won between 1956–60.

Surtees had made the switch from two to four wheels in 1959 and after winning his last world title in 1960 concentrated on cars full-time. Initially he raced his own Formula Two car but in 1962 was invited to join the Ferrari team. He had his first Grand Prix win at the Nurburgring in 1963 and, leading up to the climax of the 1964 season, had added two more wins to his tally, at the Nurburgring (again) and Monza.

One could sense the air of tension among the three leading gladiators as they arrived for practice. Clark took pole position despite having to switch from his normally reliable Lotus 25 (which developed fuel pump trouble) to the newer Lotus 33. Surtees was on the second row of the grid while Hill was one row behind.

As the race started, it was Clark who jumped away as his two rivals suffered problems at the start. Hill had trouble with his goggles while Surtees was left with a spluttering engine. At the end of lap one Clark led, with Hill in 10th place and Surtees 13th.

Both men soon overcame their problems as they went in pursuit of Clark who would win the title it he took the chequered flag with the other two out of the points.

It was Hill who offered the best challenge to the Scot and after 12 laps had pulled himself into 3rd place, a position that would give him the title if he could stay there – and keep Surtees behind him. But there was an awful lot of racing left; 53 laps to be exact, as the 'ifs and buts' continued.

At this stage it was Clark 1st, Hill 3rd, Surtees 5th. If it stayed like that then the championship would end 1 Hill, 2 Clark, 3 Surtees.

After one third of the race Clark led Dan Gurney by 10 seconds, with Hill 12 seconds behind in third, but Hill was closely pursued by the

Italian Bandini, in his Ferrari. Just before the half-way stage Bandini clipped the back of Hill's BRM. The two men skidded off the track but the Italian was capable of getting back into the race. Hill's exhaust was badly damaged and he was forced to make his way to the pits. Repairs were carried out and he re-joined the race but it was too late for him to get back into contention and he had to follow the other two title contenders from a couple of laps behind. From now on his destiny was out of his own hands.

While the Bandini–Hill scuffle was taking place Surtees moved into 3rd place. The championship now stood at: Clark 39 pts, Hill 39 pts, Surtees 38 pts. It could hardly have been closer.

Bandini's 12-cylinder Ferrari was much quicker than Surtees' V8 version, and within three laps of his spill Bandini had overtaken his team-mate and taken 3rd place.

With seven laps remaining the world title

seemed to be coming Jim Clark's way for the second successive year. He led Gurney by nearly 20 seconds and was pulling away with each lap. But then disaster – an oil pipe split. Left with no option but to carry on racing, Clark had to ease off the accelerator, a luxury he could afford with having such a big lead. But on the final lap the engine seized completely. Gurney took the lead, Bandini was 2nd and Surtees 3rd. But that was no good for the Englishman, he needed a second place to clinch the title. Bandini slowed down to let his team-mate pass and go on to take second place and the required six points to make him the first dual world champion.

Jim Clark was classified 5th even though he was not running at the finish but the two points he collected were no good to him. The final standings in one of the closest finishes to a championship season were:

1. John Surtees (Great Britain)
   Ferrari 40 points
2. Graham Hill (Great Britain)
   BRM 39 points
3. Jim Clark (Great Britian)
   Lotus 32 points

The great Jim Clark may have missed the chance of a second world title in 1964, but a year later he added a second drivers' title to the one he won in 1963. Clark was a winner, as his record of 25 wins from 72 starts shows. Coming second was no good to the man regarded as the ultimate professional. In the **1967 Italian Grand Prix** Clark finished third, one of only six such finishes for the Scot during his Grand Prix career. But his efforts that day at Monza typified the brilliance of the man as he enjoyed the 'race of his life'.

Eighteen cars lined up on that sunny Italian day, including the new Honda RA300. Under farcical conditions the race got under way: a new rule was introduced whereby the starters were to move forward at the drop of a flag. Jack Brabham misunderstood the flag and shot away. Confused, the rest of the field followed the Australian. They weren't called back and the race continued. Surprisingly, despite the false start, the drivers soon settled down.

Clark took the lead on lap 5 when he went past his Lotus team-mate Graham Hill. Brabham and Dan Gurney filled 3rd and 4th places. Four laps later Clark lost the lead to Denny Hulme who had moved through the field. But the New Zealander's lead was short-lived as Clark soon regained it.

On the 13th lap Clark had problems with one of his tyres. The wheel change took well over a minute and when he rejoined the race he was a lap behind the leaders and in 15th place. Only Jackie Stewart, who was having mechanical problems, was behind him.

The lead was now fiercely contested by Hill, Brabham and Hulme but Clark set off on one of the greatest charges seen in Grand Prix racing.

By lap 25 he had made some headway and was on the same lap as the leaders. As the race approached its half-way stage, one of the contenders, Denny Hulme, was forced out with overheating problems. After 34 of the scheduled 68 laps Clark was in seventh place and rapidly catching the bunch. He was soon to be challenging for third place.

With three-quarters of the race gone Clark caught and passed Jochen Rindt to move into 4th place. The next man in his sights was Surtees in the new Honda, which was performing well. In front of Surtees lay the race leaders, Hill and Brabham. As Clark was gaining a couple of seconds on each lap, the prospect of him catching the leaders was becoming more of a reality.

Nine laps from the finish Clark hauled back Surtees and moved into 3rd place. Almost at the same time, Clark's Lotus team-mate Graham Hill retired with engine trouble and suddenly the Scot found himself in second place. On lap 61 Clark miraculously took the lead when he slipped past Brabham. With his skill and the power of his Lotus 49, he pulled away from the field and was ready for the greatest victory since Fangio's at the Nurburgring ten years earlier.

Brabham slipped down the field and lost second place to Surtees with three laps to go, but the former motor cycling world champion never looked like coming back at Clark and the result seemed a foregone conclusion. But suddenly Clark's car spluttered, the fuel wasn't getting through. This was the one chance Surtees and Brabham had hoped for, and they seized upon Clark's misfortune.

At the start of the last lap Clark still led, but his lead had been reduced to two seconds. As they reached Lesmos, Brabham and Surtees both passed the luckless Clark. Brabham re-took the lead; Surtees got it back. In the end the Honda was first over the finish line, a mere ²/₁₀ of a second ahead of the Brabham-Repco, to give the new Japanese car a great debut win.

But spare a thought for Clark who coasted over the line in third place, 23 seconds behind the first two. After such a brilliant drive in which

he took on the entire field, a victory was the only just reward for Jim Clark's greatest ever drive.

Scotland's other great driver of the era, Jackie Stewart, also engaged in some great drives during his 99-race career. But one of his finest drives must surely have been in the rain and mist at the Nurburgring during the **1968 German Grand Prix** when, single-handed, he conquered the monster German circuit.

Appalling weather cast doubts about the running of the race, the 30th German Grand Prix. But after an hour's delay, and little sign of the rain letting up, the organisers decided to get proceedings under way.

Practice had been a farce because of the bad weather, and the grid positions bore little resemblance to the true ability of the twenty starters.

There were rivers of water all over the fourteen-mile track and the organizers allowed an extra practice session on the morning of the race to allow the drivers to find out where the rivers of water lay! One man who didn't want to take part in the final practice, or even the race itself, was Stewart. A firm believer in safety controls he felt conditions were too bad to race in, but his mentor, Ken Tyrrell, *made* him go out and race. The decision was to be fully justified as Stewart had the race of his life.

When the cars eventually lined up, Jackie Stewart started from the third row of the newly designed 3–2–3 grid. Despite his reluctance to take part, Stewart was the pre-race favourite, having won the Dutch Grand Prix in the wet six weeks earlier.

The opening lap posed numerous problems, not least for the spectators who could barely identify the cars amidst the spray. The wet created all sorts of problems for many of the cars but Stewart's Matra-Ford was fitted with special 'Super-wet' Dunlop tyres. The result was unbelievable.

After the first lap he led by nine seconds; by the end of lap 2 he had stretched the lead by a further 25 seconds. As the other drivers experienced various problems the Scot just ate up the miles of the vast circuit.

After four laps Stewart led by one minute and at the halfway mark (seven laps) he was 1½ minutes clear of the rest of the field, which saw a great battle for second place between Jacky Ickx, Jack Brabham, Graham Hill, Chris Amon and Denny Hulme.

Stewart completely dominated proceedings and the rest of the story is history. The Scot continued to pull away and in the end won by an amazing four minutes in the greatest race of his magnificent career. By the time the second car of Graham Hill could be seen coming into the finishing straight, Stewart had parked his blue Matra and was talking to friends!

Along with Monaco, the Nurburgring has been regarded as one of the biggest names among the post-war motor racing circuits. If Stewart's win at 'The Ring' in 1968 represented one of 'The biggest winning margins seen over the famous circuit, then Jochen Rindt's victory in the **1970 Monaco Grand Prix** was one of the narrowest in the long history of the famous race around the streets of Monte Carlo.

Rindt won five championship races in 1970

Left: Jackie Stewart took pole position at the 1970 Monaco Grand Prix in the March 701 and immediately took the lead. But he had to pull out 22 laps from the end to make way for the two central characters, Jack Brabham and Jochen Rindt. Rindt was the eventual winner.

Right: Peter Gethin in his P160 BRM during the 1971 Italian Grand Prix. Gethin was the winner of the closest ever world championship race.

before he lost his life in the 10th round of the championship at Monza, building up such an invincible lead that he was posthumously crowned the world champion.

Before his untimely death, he started his great run to the championship at Monaco on 10 May when he took advantage of a rare mistake by Australian Jack Brabham on the final bend and seized his chance to snatch a last-gasp victory.

Monaco has been the scene of many great battles over the years, but Rindt's victory is one of the closest in the race's long history.

The miserable weather of the practice days turned to sunshine on race day and, as always, the streets of Monte Carlo were packed with enthusiastic fans.

Reigning world champion Jackie Stewart was in pole position, while the men who were to become the race's central characters, Brabham and Rindt, were on the second and fourth rows respectively of the 16-car grid. The Scot led from the start until ignition problems started on lap 27. A four-minute pit-stop did his chances no good whatsoever, and while he was receiving repairs Jack Brabham took the lead with New Zealander Chris Amon second and Denny Hulme third. It was an Australasian 1–2–3 while Henri Pescarolo and Jochen Rindt battled it out for fourth place.

Just after the half-way stage Rindt was in third place having passed Pescarolo and Hulme. There were 39 laps left but there was no giveway among the leading drivers and they held their positions until the 61st lap when Amon was forcd out of the race with suspension problems. So, with 19 laps remaining it was Brabham 1st, Rindt 2nd.

With four laps to go Brabham had a nine second lead – a big gap at Monte Carlo. Coming through the Casino Square three laps from home Brabham was hampered by Siffert while trying to overtake the Swiss driver. This gave Rindt the chance to gain four seconds. But, with three laps to go, the Austrian still had to make up a further five seconds; a tall order at Monte.

But the fearless Rindt pushed himself and his Lotus to the limit and as Rindt and Brabham went into the tunnel for the last time there was less than a second between the two as the chequered flag beckoned.

After lapping Piers Courage going into the Gasworks bend the Australian braked too late and went into the straw bales. Rindt leapt like a predator after his prey and grabbed the lead to take the flag. Brabham came in nearly 18 seconds later, sadly beaten into second place in one of the most dramatic finishes ever seen in the Monaco Grand Prix.

If the 1970 Monaco Grand Prix was won by sheer opportunism following a driving error then the **1971 Italian Grand Prix** at Monza was won by sheer staying power and the width of a few cigarette papers at the end of an amazing 196 mile (316km) race.

Only six-tenths of a second separated the first five drivers at the end of the closest race in the history of the world championship.

Clay Regazzoni was the early leader in his Ferrari but there was a feeling he would soon lose that lead and indeed, on lap 4 that is what happened when Ronnie Peterson took control in his March. But he was closely followed by the likes of Jackie Stewart, Peter Gethin, Francois Cevert, Jo Siffert and Jacky Ickx. The lead constantly changed, with Peterson's March at the front more often than the others. However, with only one second between the leaders, the lead had little significance at this stage.

After 16 laps it was goodbye to both Stewart and Ickx who went out with mechanical problems. And not long afterwards they were joined by the one-time leader Regazzoni. The lead was still a constantly changing affair, this time between Peterson, Cevert and Mike Hailwood new to the fray at the front of the field.

Hailwood took the lead on lap 25 and, as the race passed the half-way stage, it was Siffert who took control. A few laps later he dropped back with gearbox trouble. The slightest hiccup meant a drop of half-a-dozen places. The battle was that tight.

Peterson, Cevert and Hailwood were still the front runners but on lap 37 Chris Amon overtook all three to become the new race leader. At the same time Peter Gethin was making a move. For ten laps Amon held the lead and for the first time a possible winner was emerging. But then he made the mistake of attempting to remove one of his visors. The whole system came away and the decision cost Amon dearly as suddenly he dropped back into sixth position.

The five drivers in front of him – Peterson, Hailwood, Cevert, Gethin and Howden Ganley – were separated by less than two seconds. They pulled away from Amon even further and the one-time winner was suddenly drifting from the leading pack.

Gethin slipped past the other four to take the lead on lap 52. With three laps remaining, and with such a close contest behind him, the outcome was still uncertain. Gethin held on to the lead, but any of the other four were still capable of snatching a last-gasp win. The lead changed hands again and going into the Parabolica for the last time it was Cevert who led the others through. But he then made a mistake. He

Above: Peter Gethin during the closest Grand Prix on record when ⁶/₁₀ of a second separated the first five drivers.

Right: Emerson Fittipaldi in the McLaren M23 finished fourth at Watkins Glen but it was good enough to give him a second world title.

braked late and Peterson went past him. But the Swede went too wide and Cevert and Gethin went past on the inside. Gethin got his BRM up to cross the line first and record his first, and only, championship success. Peterson came back at Cevert to snatch second place, while Hailwood took fourth.

So this is how the first five finished in the closest of all Grand Prix races:

Gethin's winning speed was 150.75mph (242.62kph) which makes it the fastest Grand Prix of all time.

While the speed of the 1971 Italian Grand Prix made it one of the most exciting in recent memory, there can be little to match the atmosphere surrounding the final race of a season in which the outcome of the world championship still has to be decided.

1. Peter Gethin	Great Britian	BRM	1h 18m 12.60s
2. Ronnie Peterson	Sweden	March-Ford	1h 18m 12.61s
3. Francois Cevert	France	Tyrrell-Ford	1h 18m 12.69s
4. Mike Hailwood	Great Britain	Surtees-Ford	1h 18m 12.78s
5. Howden Ganley	New Zealand	BRM	1h 18m 13.21s

Above left: Nelson Piquet in the Brabham takes advantage of his pole position to reach the first bend in front of the rest of the field at Estoril in 1984.

In 1984 Marlboro-McLaren comfortably won the Constructors' Championship but the drivers' title came down to the last race at Estoril. Alain Prost (*left*) won the final round of the championship but, by following him home in second place, Niki Lauda (*top right*) did enough, by a mere half a point, to assure his third world title.

Middle right: The all-conquering Marlboro-McLaren team.

Bottom right: Prost, Lauda and Senna.

We have already seen in 1958 how the championship went to a dramatic conclusion at Casablanca when it went to the very last lap. But there have been other equally eventful climaxes to other championship seasons in recent years.

The **1974 United States Grand Prix** at Watkins Glen was to decide the outcome of that year's championship after an already gruelling fourteen race schedule. The 250th Grand Prix since the start of the world championship in 1950, it was perhaps appropriate that it should mark the climax to a very close season that was not decided until the final round at 'The Glen'.

Clay Regazzoni and Emerson Fittipaldi shared the championship lead with 52 points while South African Jody Scheckter was still in with a chance on 45 points. None of the title contenders was on the first two rows of the grid; Scheckter was on row three, Fittipaldi on row four, and Regazzoni on row five.

The twenty-four drivers set off in bright sunshine and the first half of the race was dominated by Carlos Reutemann, James Hunt and Carlos Pace. Scheckter and Fittipaldi were in touch with the leaders but Regazzoni was having problems controlling his Ferrari.

An accident on lap 10 marred the race when Austrian Helmuth Koinigg was killed after his Surtees careered off the track.

On lap 45 Scheckter was forced out of the championship with a broken fuel pipe. Regazzoni, however, while still running, had no chance of getting among the points and so the title was handed to Fittipaldi. He didn't even need the points; his 52, although the same as Regazzoni's tally, was enough for the title because he had three wins to the Swiss driver's one. And so, another world title was decided in the last race of the season. It may not have gone to the last lap, but it was only 14 laps from the end of the

Left: The cars awaiting the start of the 1974 United States Grand Prix, the 250th world championship race. The result of the 1974 Drivers' Championship hinged on the outcome of this race and the title eventually went to Brazilian Emerson Fittipaldi.

Top right: The rain-soaked Fuji International speedway shortly after the start of the 1976 Japanese Grand Prix. Niki Lauda pulled out of the race on lap two and that paved the way for Britain's James Hunt to win the world championship . . . which he did.

Bottom right: It was still raining at the end of the 1976 Japanese Grand Prix as American Mario Andretti took the chequered flag, but the world title went to James Hunt who finished third.

season that Emerson Fittipaldi knew with confidence that he was going to lift his second world title.

Two years later the **1976 Japanese Grand Prix** at Fuji provided an even more dramatic climax to an exciting season. In the nine months since the first race of the season at Brazil, there had been a succession of dramas, controversies, disqualifications, reinstatements, and an horrific accident to Niki Lauda at Nurburgring which almost claimed his life.

Lauda was well on his way to his second world title when he had his accident at 'The Ring' in August. Being out of action, Britain's James Hunt took advantage and hauled himself into a championship-winning position. Little did he know at the time that Lauda was making a dramatic recovery and was to get back into his car before the season was out.

Less than six weeks after his accident in Ger-

many, Lauda was racing again, and finished fourth at Monza. Hunt failed to pick up any points in Italy, but did win the next two races at Mosport and Watkins Glen. As the 16th and final round approached, Lauda led the championship with 68 points to Hunt's 65, and so the final battle was to be fought in Japan, the first time the championship had gone to the Land of the Rising Sun.

In practice Hunt in his McLaren and Lauda in his Ferrari were 2nd and 3rd fastest after Mario Andretti's JPS-Lotus. Weather conditions were very wet and visibility was down to around 100 yards (110m). After two laps it was apparent Lauda had other things on his mind than racing as driver after driver went past him. He pulled in at the end of the second lap and indicated his withdrawal from the race because he felt conditions were too dangerous. Effectively he had handed the championship to Hunt. Many criti-

Right: Nigel Mansell in the Williams on the front row of the grid for the 1986 Spanish Grand Prix at Jerez. Unfortunately he was pipped by the narrowest of margins by Ayrton Senna at the end of 189 miles (319km) of racing.

Below: Pits action involving the two McLarens at Jerez in 1986. But it was the Lotus of Ayrton Senna and the Williams of Nigel Mansell who battled it out for the chequered flag with the Brazilian taking it by $14/1000$ of a second. Victory in Spain would have given the world championship to Nigel six months later.

cized the Austrian's action, but he obviously still had the Nurburgring on his mind, and one man who didn't condemn Lauda's decision was his team boss Enzo Ferrari.

James Hunt had been in the lead for most of the race. He needed only to finish 4th or better to take the title; a win wasn't necessary.

As he held on to his lead the rain stopped and the track dried out. This may have been advantageous to the large crowd who could dispense with umbrellas and plastic raincoats, but it posed problems to the race leader's tyres.

With 20 laps remaining, the wet-weather tyres of Hunt's McLaren were overheating and one of his front tyres was badly worn. The decision to pull him in for new tyres might prove costly; neither the pits, nor Hunt himself would make the decision to come in, so he kept going.

To lighten the burden on the tyres Hunt eased up on the throttle; this allowed Patrick Depailler and Mario Andretti to make ground. With 11 laps to go, Hunt was passed by those two. He was now third and still in world championship position, but would he stay there?

On lap 67, and with 6 laps left Hunt's tyre eventually gave way and ended up a shredded mess. As luck would have it, the disaster happened in front of the pits and he went in for a wheel change. Four new tyres were put on and the change, a long one at nearly thirty seconds, seemed like a lifetime to British supporters. How long must it have felt to Hunt?

With 4 laps left Hunt was 5th and out of the championship. Fortunately for Hunt, Alan Jones and 'Clay Regazzoni in front of him were now suffering similar tyre problems and they were forced to slow down. This gave Hunt the opportunity to overtake them both on the penultimate lap and move into third place. Just over a minute later it was all over. Mario Andretti crossed the line first, followed by Depailler then Hunt.

Hunt was unaware that he had clinched the title. He thought he was too low down the finishing order and was ready to remonstrate with his McLaren team for not calling him in for a tyre change. Suddenly, it was pointed out to him that he was world champion. The threatened confrontation was thwarted and the champagne started flowing as Britain celebrated her first world champion since Jackie Stewart three years earlier.

In 1967 Britain's Jim Clark was to have the misfortune of running out of petrol after giving the performance of his life during the Italian Grand Prix. Ten years later another Briton, John Watson, suffered the same fate during the **1977 French Grand Prix** at Dijon, after also giving one of the finest performances of his career.

Watson had his first Grand Prix win at the Osterreichring during James Hunt's championship year. But in 1977 he had done very little of note. In fact, he arrived at Dijon with only three points to his credit after finishing 6th at Kyalami and 5th at Anderstorp. But after an hour and a half's racing around the recently extended French circuit, John Watson was to emerge from the cockpit of his Brabham a shattered and disappointed man after narrowly missing out on his second Grand Prix win.

As the first Grand Prix at Dijon since 1974 got under way, reigning world champion James Hunt in his McLaren and Watson in his Brabham-Alfa had great starts. Mario Andretti, who shared the front row of the grid with Hunt, had a bad start and lost ground immediately.

By the time the field had settled down it was Hunt, Watson and Andretti who pulled away from the rest of the field. On the 5th lap the Irishman came out of Hunt's slipstream to take the lead. Hunt was then engaged in a great battle with Andretti for second place.

Andretti got the better of the Englishman for the first time on the 17th lap, but he was five seconds behind the leader Watson. From now on, the race was to be a two-car battle between the Brabham and Andretti's JPS-Lotus.

After 40 of the 72 laps Andretti started closing the gap slightly when the Briton was caught up among some back-markers. On lap 50 Watson's lead was down to three seconds, but he was still driving superbly. Ten laps later the two cars were virtually level. Behind them a lot of ill-feeling was being generated by Watson's teammate, the German Hans Stuck, who wouldn't let the local hero Jacques Laffite through, despite a lot of blue flag-waving from the marshals.

As the race reached its conclusion, and with just two laps remaining, Watson still held off the American driver; Andretti just couldn't find a way past.

Watson was driving brilliantly and Andretti was, by now, utterly frustrated and was resigned to collecting the runners-up 6 points. At the start of the last lap the pattern of the previous 20 looked set to follow with Watson fending off his pursuer. At the top of the new loop the Brabham suddenly spluttered; it was running out of fuel. Andretti had been waiting for a chance like this and he took it. He pulled level with the Brabham, and when Watson's car spluttered again, Andretti was past him in a flash.

The Lotus took the chequered flag while Watson cruised home to take second place, with James Hunt a further 30 seconds behind third.

The battle between Watson and Andretti was a memorable one. The Briton made no mistakes but was punished in the cruellest of ways. At the end he was dreadfully unlucky and bitterly disappointed. His disappointment was shared by most of the French fans that July day at Dijon.

Nelson Piquet won his first world title in 1981 when he snatched the title in the last race of the season, around the car park of the Caesar's Palace complex in Las Vegas. The **1983 South African Grand Prix** was to be the setting of his second title win and again he snatched it in the last race of the season. Piquet went into the race two points adrift of Alain Prost, with another Frenchman, Rene Arnoux, in with an outside chance if Prost and Piquet failed to get among the points, which is what had happened at Zandvoort six weeks earlier.

Above left: Mario Andretti in the *John Player Special* Lotus. Andretti was the man who deprived Britain's John Watson of a memorable win at Dijon-Prenois.

Above right: Andrea de Cesaris (Italy) in the Marlboro-sponsored Alfa Romeo during the 1983 South African Grand Prix, where he equalled his best ever Grand Prix finish, 2nd.

Right: Kyalami 1983 was a happy place to be for this Brabham pair – Patrese (*right*) won the race while third place was enough for Piquet to snatch the world title from Alain Prost (France).

The final practice session however saw another Frenchman, Patrick Tambay, take pole position. A Ferrari team-mate of Arnoux, he had been sacked by Ferrari for 1984 but was determined to go out in a blaze of personal glory.

Piquet in his Brabham, took an early lead, and on lap 9 the first of his challengers, Arnoux, pulled out of the race with his Ferrari losing power.

The Brazilian brilliantly controlled the race from the front and on lap 29 came in for a pit stop that was so quick (a record 9.2 sec) he re-turned to the race in first place. Fourteen laps later Prost's Renault came in for its fuel and tyre stop. The pit stop lasted 45 seconds. Two laps later Prost pulled out of the race; the long pit stop and his quest to keep up with Piquet took its toll on the Renault's engine and the turbo-charger let him down.

With his two rivals out of the race Piquet had the world at his feet and needed only to finish 4th or better. But his car was obviously in trou-ble. His Brabham team-mate Patrese passed him

Top left: The victory salute that says it all: Alain Prost (France) after retaining his world title at Adelaide in the final race of the 1986 season that brought an end to one of the closest world championships.

Left: The Brabhams of Patrese and Warwick in the lead at Adelaide, but keeping a careful watch on proceedings are the McLaren duo of Prost and Rosberg.

Centre: Out on his own and just needing to stay there to clinch the title . . . and that is just what Alain Prost did at Adelaide in 1986.

Top right: Mansell 1, Prost 2. if it had stayed like that then Nigel Mansell would have been Britain's first world champion since 1976.

Right: The smile says it all: "I'm world champion again."

after holding the lead for 60 of the 77 laps. And Niki Lauda, having his best race of the season in the new Marlboro-McLaren, was catching him fast. But lap 71 saw Lauda's car fall victim to the intense heat and 6,000-feet altitude as he ground to a halt. But as Lauda dropped out, Piquet had a new challenger in Andrea de Cesaris in his Alfa Romeo. The Italian pushed Piquet into third place on lap 75. The Brazilian was now grimly holding on to the world title in his failing car.

However, Piquet managed to hold on and come in behind Patrese and de Cesaris to get the four points that took him to the world title for the second time and thus deprive Alain Prost of becoming the first French world champion. Nelson Piquet, 6,000-feet up at Kyalami, was certainly on top of the world once more.

Twelve months later Alain Prost failed yet again to become the first French world champion. This time the margin of defeat was even less as his McLaren team-mate Niki Lauda won the title by a meagre half-a-point in a great finish to the season.

Not since the early days of the world championship had one team dominated the series as Marlboro-McLaren did in 1984 (they did so again in 1988) when they won 12 of the 16 championship rounds, but the most crucial was the championship-decider on 21 October, the **1984 Portuguese Grand Prix** at Estoril; Portugal's first Grand Prix for twenty-four years.

After winning the Italian Grand Prix at Monza, Lauda looked certain to win his third world title, but Prost picked up maximum points at the New Nurburgring in the next race, the European Grand Prix, to stay in contention. Going into the final race Prost expected to be trailing Lauda by 4½ points but just before the Portuguese race he received an unexpected bonus of an extra championship point following Martin Brundle's disqualification from the Detroit Grand Prix. So, with Prost on the front row of the starting grid at Estoril, and Lauda struggling on the 6th row, just 3½ points separated the two McLaren drivers.

Prost took the lead on lap nine when he went past the Williams of Keke Rosberg. The Frenchman was not to lose that lead over the remaining 61 laps. But winning was to be no good to Prost if Lauda finished second, because it would mean a third world title to the Austrian.

Lauda kept picking off opponents as he strove for that second place position behind Prost. On lap 33 he moved into third place and when Britain's Nigel Mansell made a pit stop on lap 51 Lauda took over the second place that would guarantee him the championship. Prost knew

what was going on behind him but was powerless to do anything. He could only carry on and win and watch as his team-mate followed him over the line to secure the coveted world title.

Alain Prost missed out on the world title for the second year running and this time by the narrowest of margins. Happily, the Frenchman has now added his name to the list of great men who have won the title, not once, but twice.

When Prost won his second world title in 1986 it was in dramatic fashion once more, as he came from behind to overhaul Nigel Mansell in the last race of the season. But seven months earlier, Mansell was engaged in one of the closest Grand Prix races of all time when he was pipped by Ayrton Senna by 0.014 of a second in the **1986 Spanish Grand Prix** at Jerez.

From lap 40 it developed into a battle between the Lotus of Senna, the Williams of Mansell and the McLaren of Prost. With 10 laps to go Mansell was dealt a blow when a slow puncture meant a pit stop. He rejoined the race in third place and set off at a blistering pace. He gained two seconds on every lap on the two leaders and on lap 69 Prost and Mansell engaged in an intense battle for second place; Mansell won.

Mansell's new tyres certainly made a difference but as the chequered flag approached, the British driver 'ran out of race' with Senna being caught all the time. The Brazilian crossed the line first as Mansell needed another 20 yards (18.2m) to get his Williams in front.

The battle for second place with Prost on lap 69 cost Mansell a few seconds. As Senna won by $^{14}/_{1000}$ths of a second, it was indeed valuable time lost.

Nigel Mansell's Spanish disappointment was overcome later in the season when he won the Belgian, Canadian, French, British and Portuguese Grands Prix and put himself on course to become Britain's first world champion since James Hunt ten years earlier.

The climax of the sixteen-race season was at Adelaide on 26 October for the **1986 Australian Grand Prix**. Mansell was the championship-leader on 70 points, while Prost and Piquet each had 63. To take the title the Briton only needed to finish third or better. However, if any driver other than Prost or Piquet won the race then the title would still be Mansell's, irrespective of where he finished.

In the fifteen races that preceded Adelaide, Mansell had finished in the first three no less than nine times. But, racing is a funny game . . .

The McLarens of Keke Rosberg (having his last race), and Alain Prost dominated the race. Following a minor collision Prost damaged a front tyre and went into the pits on lap 33. The

Goodyear technicians took the opportunity to examine the tyres and gave a 'thumbs up' which indicated that Rosberg's would last the full distance. But with three-quarters of the race run, and leading by 30 seconds, Rosberg lost a large chunk of tread coming down the fast Brabham straight.

A minute-and-a-half later, and just before Williams called Mansell and team-mate Piquet in for tyre checks, the left-rear tyre of Mansell's car disintegrated, and so did his world championship hopes. The Briton did remarkably well to control his car and thus avoid a major disaster as he steered it to safety. He survived without injury, except a broken heart as millions of Briton's shared his anguish.

He could only stand and watch the remainder of the race which saw Prost and Piquet battle it out for the race and championship. Both honours went to the Frenchman who, once again, was involved in a great climax to a great season, thus bringing to an end another great race in a long list of memorable Grands Prix over the last thirty-eight years.

Fangio taking the chequered flag in the 250F Maserati. It was one of four victories for the Argentinian in 1957 as he won his fifth and final world drivers' title.

Index

Page numbers in italics refer to illustrations.